the *LAST* POST

...or how to build the Heysen Trail in 400 years or less

by **Terry Lavender**

BOOKENDS
BOOKS

First published 2001 by:
Bookend Books, 136 Unley Rd, Unley South Australia
email: bookends.bookshop@adelaide.on.net

Editor
Rob Scott

Design:
John Hyland (Plan Pink Design)

Cartoons:
Bill Sheridan

Photographs:
Terry Lavender
Andrew Moylan

Printing
Hyde Park Press

Lavender, Terry.
The last post.

Bibliography.
ISBN 1 876725 01 X.

1. Trails - South Australia. 2. Heysen Trail (S. Aust.).
I. Sheridan, Bill. II. Moylan, Andrew. III. Title.

796.51099423

**BOOKENDS
BOOKS**

Contents

Foreward

I gained a unique understanding of the impact Terry Lavender's influence has on the lives of many South Australians when I was returning to Adelaide on an overseas flight. Prior to landing there was Terry on the video screens extolling the virtues of South Australia.

Yes, it came to me, Terry is the right South Australian to welcome people to our state. He is very Adelaide. The ideal person to convey the special beauty of the scenery of South Australia to our visitors. He is comfortably at home in his Akubra hat and bush clothes. He is an easily met friendly person.

Terry is known as the 'Father of the Heysen Trail', the 1500km walking trail regarded by many as their favourite South Australian asset. The Heysen Trail has introduced walking as a recreation to thousands of South Australians who would never have known where they could legally and safely go for a walk in the bush.

Until the inception of the trail, bushwalking was pretty much confined to a few hardy souls carrying big rucksacks while wearing short pants and big boots.

It was Terry who planned the route, visited the landowners and convinced country councillors that a walking trail is a desirable amenity in their districts.

It was Terry who got out there with the volunteer marking teams putting in the first, the middle and the last posts showing the route of the Heysen Trail. Along the way there were tangles with bureaucracy, an uplifting contact with a visionary and wary landholders to convince. There were all manner of farm gates to negotiate, threatening cattle dogs to be ignored and an unplanned night in the bush.

This is Terry's account of how the Heysen Trail came into being. It is told in his easy speaking style, straightforward but with the art of the raconteur.

The Last Post is an immensely entertaining read.

George Driscoll

George Driscoll is the Manager of the Snowgum Outdoor Centre in Rundle Street, Adelaide. He is a Churchill Fellow having studied the retailing of Outdoor Goods around the world. George is the author of '50 Real Bushwalks around Adelaide', now in it's 4th edition. He is co-editor of a bushwalking cook-book 'The Lightweight Cooks'. George is the founder and life member of the Pathfinder Walking Group and a member of the Friends of the Heysen Trail.

This book is dedicated to
Stella Salter and Ann Lavender, for without
their skills, patience and enthusiasm it would
still just be a good idea.

Introduction

South Australia must be the best State in the Commonwealth for
walking. With its moderate climate abundance of scenic attractions,
rugged arid mountain ranges, lush rolling hills and ancient ragged coast line.
From the forests of the South east to the mighty Flinders Ranges, South
Australia is the State for walkers.

Most countries have a long distance recreation trail. The North
Americans in particular have been smitten with them which is no bad thing
when you look at their baronial system of land tenure. We have all seen in
recent years the lengths some United States citizens are prepared to go to
preserve the integrity of their property. The Pacific Crest Trail which runs
down the west coast of the USA is over 3000km long and even crosses
the U.S.A./Canadian border. It is of course a dual use trail on which both
walkers, horses and horse riders are allowed. The British, who not only
believe that God is an Englishman, also, believe that they invented bushwalking, and well they might I can think of no better claimant. They have
over 120,000km of footpaths, track ways, bridle paths, green roads, hollow
ways and tow paths. From the Longships Light to Hadrian's Wall it is
possible to walk on almost every piece of Albion. Throughout the world
there are numerous long distance trails. It is now possible to follow
Hannibal's route over the Alps, wander the Himalayas, follow in the foot
steps of Major Mitchell and even traverse Hong Kong Island on the unlikely
named MacLeod Trail and the New Zealanders have had the Milford Track
for years, yes we are all at it, and in South Australia we did it this way.

*Fence Posts, dead tress and stumps were
all candidates for marker posts*

National Fitness Council

had been at the National Fitness Council (NFC) since early 1971, and it was pretty much my ideal job. I was responsible for the NFC outdoor recreation leadership training program and was working at the National Fitness Council when I first heard of the Heysen Trail; sometime about 1972 or 73. Albert Simpson the Director of the Council was a rep. on the Long Distance Trails Committee. I was not asked until much later, even though I was responsible for the development of the Council's network of trails in the Mt Lofty Ranges, a network of over 800kms. This was probably because of my opposition to the concept of the Long Distance Trail, although this was never said. I had by this time got to know the local ranges quite well and had become deeply impressed by them and by the way they gave little hint of their beauty and drama from the plains. The recreational possibilities seemed to me huge particularly given their proximity to the great majority of the State's population. It seemed to me that to spend $1,000,000 of the public's hard earned money for the pleasure of a few dedicated walkers was not good management. I held the view that a network of trails in the hills close to Adelaide would be a lot more effective way of spending the money, and so I did not have much to do with the Heysen Trail until 1978. Warren Bonython has written that early history and it is still available from the Friends of the Heysen Trail.

I ran two youth camps each year, a two week aquatics camp at Clayton Bay, and a mountain activities training camp in the Flinders Ranges based on Clem Smith's property in Kangaroo Gap. So I had plenty of climbing, caving, walking, sailing, off road driving, the odd country and interstate business trip, so life was very, very good, but as they say when things are that good someone is certain to come along and stuff it up, and that someone came in the exalted guise of Gough Whitlam. In 1974 I had dinner with Gough at the Lakeside Hotel in Canberra, me and 700 others that is, at least I was told the Prime Minister was there. We were at a conference called 'Leisure a New Perspective'. It was just at that time when Gough decided to see how quickly he could spend all our money. Apart from the NFC delegates there were representatives from South Australia, Alex Macdonald (National Parks), Tony Boulton (Salisbury CAE) and Dave Brodure (the State Planning Authority). As far as the conference dinner was concerned we seemed to be ranked by state in the order that Canberra public servants rated our importance, which meant of course that the prime seats were taken by the ACT and NSW followed closely by Queensland, we were well below the salt at a dimly lit table by the lift well inspection shaft, where we got brief glimpses of Victorian backs. We contented ourselves with feeling superior to the Tasmanians who sat in perpetual twilight at the lower end of our table. What with the sound of the wind piping up and down the lift shaft and the subdued lighting, my imagination soon had me back on a windswept winters peak in North Wales. Then someone was shouting 'stand up, stand up'. I think it was Albert Simpson, very annoyed that we hadn't done so spontaneously. Apparently Gough had entered the hall. We ate the lobsters, oysters, prawns, caviar, venison and drank the wines. There was plenty of everything. Whitlam began to speak, not that we could hear much more than a far off drone which rose and fell. Not wishing to appear impolite we nodded when the distant New South Welshmen nodded, we laughed along with the Queenslanders and sighed with the Victorians and every now and again gave a chuckle all of our own as though we had caught some hidden witticism that everyone else had missed. The crowd rose swirling and eddying around Gough like a midnight tide and he was gone.

The conference was a huge success and we all left Canberra a week later, inspired and looking forward to the new perspective. Not much happened for a while and I settled back into the varied life of an NFC field officer. Sometime later the Government announced its strategy, which was basically very simple. For the first time in the Commonwealth's history the Federal Government would take responsibility for recreation and sport and do this by the simple expedient of making grants to the States. There was a sting in the tail however, the money would not be available to community groups or statutory authorities, in other words State Governments would have to create a specific ministerial portfolio to receive the cash. The good old NFC was therefore doomed. The Council's staff most of whom were hard working and loyal, were now treated badly. We were never told directly of our future. We were simply allowed to find it out bit by bit as the facts leaked out. Things did not look at all bright. We were not public servants and there would be no guarantee of becoming one, we would however be able to apply for positions in the new ministry if they became available. It was decided not to close the NFC until the director, Albert Simpson reached retiring age. So for a time the new Department of Tourism, Recreation and Sport with Tom Casey the Minister of Agriculture adding the new portfolio to his present responsibilities, and Bill Ispell a long serving old school public servant, as Director, continued to operate it at the same time. The Ministry began to appoint staff and things didn't look too good for us. I applied for a position as a recreation officer but was rejected despite many years of experience and considerable success in the field. However salvation was at hand as Don Dunstan, South Australia's Premier at the time, heard of our plight and typical of the man seeing an injustice about to be done came to our rescue.

We were not to be cast aside, positions would be found for all those who wanted them, somewhere in the Public Service. I received an offer of a job in the National Parks and Wildlife Service, an offer I was very pleased to get as the little I had seen of the Dept. Rec and Sport did not impress me. The offer was working for Ross Gobbey a West Australian who had been involved with the early development of the Bibulman Track. I was to be responsible for the development of trails throughout the National Parks and act as the liaison between outdoor recreation groups some who were not getting on very well with Parks authorities, mainly due to a lack of communication. I even got as far as being given a desk and phone and allocated a vehicle, but the ranger staff bucked at this. It was a good job and they wanted it to go to one of them, and so I was back on offer again. There was no escape this time. On a bright morning in the middle of 1978 I reported for duty on the 9th floor of the Black Stump in Grenfell Street as a recreation officer level 3, the lowest possible rank they could appoint me, and well below the level to which other

Making some impact

officers were being appointed. I was not wanted here, I was not the right stuff and they were determined to show me. But it was a job and well enough paid and I could bide my time, and I had to. It was over four years before my position as a public servant was confirmed. I worked for the Public Service of South Australia for 25 years the first 24 of which were great years, productive, creative happy and well paid. I was for the most part given support for the work I wanted to do and was well enough treated, I did manage to progress through the ranks although it was always a battle royal to do so. I went much further than any one including myself ever thought possible. I was the manager of Recreation S A the Department's recreation division and was the acting director for much of that time. How come then you will find criticism of the Public Service in this saga? Well perhaps I am just another whingeing pom!

The Public Service Board of South Australia seemed to be more interested in change than it was in serving the community. I started out at The Dept. of Tourism Recreation and Sport, which became the Dept. of Community Development, The Division of Recreation and Sport, The South Australian Recreation Institute, Recreation SA and finally The Office of Recreation, Sport and Racing. During my time at the Dept. we had 11 people in the top position variously titled Director, CE, General Manager and EO The Dept. had 8 Ministers, offices at 6 locations. Each new CEO wanted change, we were

reviewed, restructured reorganised. We had Award Restructuring, Enterprise Bargaining, Development Plans, Business Plans, Strategic Plans, 3 Year Plans, 5 Year Plans, Risk management, Asset Management, and Team Management. In the meantime all we had to do was to develop the world's longest footpath, avoiding the office politics, which in the atmosphere created by the above was inevitable.

Jim Daly was the senior recreation officer at the time I started and it was to him that I reported that fateful morning. He told me that they really didn't have any thing for me to do and there were no outdoor recreation funds. He asked me to write a paper describing what I was going to do. Sod that!! I gave it a few weeks during which I was given a mixed bag

Erosion control near Kapunda

of jobs and then went back to him and put this proposition to him. The NFC trails, all 800kms of them, were still popular and needed maintaining. The workshop was still in existence and there was a stock of waymarkers and other assorted trail furniture, plus an ancient panel van. Give me the responsibility for maintaining the trails. Jim agreed, I think he was relieved and glad to be rid of me, and so once more it was back to the bush and one more step down fate's path towards my destiny as the developer of the Heysen Trail.

The next Monday I left the office, picked up the van, signs and tools from the ex NFC workshop, somehow I'd forgotten to give back the key, and headed for the Mt Crawford forest where I spent the day in splendid isolation, saw no one all day and did not set off back to the City until late in the afternoon. So it was that at about 4 o'clock I was driving down the Main North road when I came in sight of my home, well almost. The temptation was too great, the thought of steaming cups of English Breakfast and hot buttered crumpets proved too much. Lamb stew and dumplings delayed me further until it was well past the time that the office would be closed. I decided to go in the next morning. Next morning this didn't seem such a good idea I wondered what the Public Service attitude to AWOL staff would be. The old NFC had allowed its officers plenty of latitude providing you got results. I suspected that the Public Service would take a different view. I did what any red blooded Aussie would do – I went back to Mt Crawford and decided to face the music later that day. It was a marvellous day, cool and very clear. I went over the Barossa Range. The valley was just stirring out of its winter sleep there was a touch of bright new green about the vines and the fresh spring grasses contrasting with the rich chocolate of newly ploughed fields. I surprised a Wegdetailed eagle tucking into a young rabbit, and later met Ian Ross the owner of the property, a splendid man who will feature later in the story of the Heysen Trail. Now I had to bite the bullet and return to the office. I rode the lift to the 9th floor expecting to be summoned to the supreme authority. The receptionist ignored me, there was no stern note in my pigeon hole, and my desk was not harbouring an urgent summons calling me before my betters. I hung about wanting the thing resolved, presently Jim Daly came out of his office, passed me by with cheerful "G'day Terry how did it go?" "Fine" I replied, "great" commented Jim and passed out into the lift and home. The die was cast, the ground rules had been laid.

From now on I would come and go as I pleased. The truth was I was much less of an embarrassment out of the office than in. The next year was spent in the Ranges, maintaining the old NFC trails and continuing to liaise with landowners. Inevitably the supply of materials ran out, I continued to roam the Mt Lofties, investigating parks, forests, road, stone, and water reserves. I spent time with Terry Pomaroy in the Roads Unit of the Lands Dept., spoke to the Pastoral Board, Local Government Association, farmers, graziers, foresters and rangers.

I was able to get staff for much of the time without difficulty. Even back in those far off times, South Australia suffered the scourge of unemployment, the difference then being that Governments did really care about people and made some effort to do something about it. To this end Don Dunstan sold the S.A. Railways to the Federal Government, a master stroke. If you had ever travelled on that ancient ramshackle shambling system you would understand just what a brilliant salesman the bloke was. The funds from the sale went into unemployment relief schemes and what with the addition of Federal monies there were always funding to be bid for and this I did as often as possible The schemes came thick and fast each with its own acronym. There was RED, SURS, SWEET PEA, SPUD and TURD. It was largely through these programs that I kept the old NFC trails going, There was opposition from within. It was one of the rules set by the givers of the funds that should there be more than one application from a department, the CEO should rank them in order of importance to the organization. Now there was within Rec. and Sport some self evident truths. Sport was overwhelmingly more important than any other activity, even watching someone else playing sport was of greater value than an active recreation. Most funding must be spent on sport or watching sport or eulogizing sports persons, even if this meant spending 90% of the available taxpayers money on a few elite sports persons. It was very un-Australian to suggest or even think that this should not be so. Sport always had to have the first crack at any additional support that might be forthcoming. Within the Recreation unit they also had a pecking order. I was still very much an outsider and spending so much time away from the office did not help. I avoided the office politics, never really understood it but knew that I was at the bottom of the pile and therefore any project that I was associated with would rank at the lowest part of the Dept anatomy. So that when applications were put in, the trails were always given the lowest priority. Despite this I was always successful, much to the chagrin of other recreation staff who rarely were.

As a result of the these successful applications, I often had a staff of six with myself as supervisor and a vehicle. I had resumed occupancy of the old NFC workshops at 70 South Terrace, Adelaide. Quite an upmarket address for such an ad hoc group as we were. Richard Massey joined the staff from one of these schemes, became the supervisor and was later put on the Department's permanent staff as the trails supervisor. Richard was a qualified psychiatric staff nurse, who, as he so eloquently put it, had become fed up with feeding faces and wiping bums and had taken a six month grand tour of NSW and Queensland, returning to South Australia happy but broke, vowing never to work as nurse again. So by a series of unplanned events he came to work for the State Government. Richard's inventiveness plus his enthusiasm for the project was going to prove invaluable over the next five years.

I was at last asked to join the Long Distance Trails Committee under the chairmanship of Warren Bonython. I went on two field trips with Dave Brodure and Rick Teague.

The Long Distance Trails Committee had some very good members but seemed unable to agree on a route through the Mt Lofties, in all only 7kms were established in the 9 year life of the committee.

I amused myself in idle moments designing a pilot trail between Mt Magnificent and Mt Lofty. I knew the country, had met most of the land managers and believed an interesting trail was possible. As it turned out this was a piece of luck, one that became very useful.

There was much during my time as a public servant that I never fully understood. The Public Service Board as it was then, was like no other employer I had ever worked for before. It stood entirely aloof from the work force. I knew one chap who had spent his whole working life there. When he finally left there was no gold

The 800 km Heysen Trail . . . only 10 km have been completed.

TRAIL BLAZING AT PACE OF A SNAIL

At its present construction rate, the Heysen Trail will be completed in the year 2376.

790 km. to go!

The 800 km riding and walking trail from Mount Babbage in the Flinders Ranges to Cape Jervis was announced in 1970.

On May 1 the Governor, Sir Mark Oliphant, will open the first 10 km between Crafers and Greenhill road.

It is an outstanding asset, but the question is where does it go from here?

It has taken five years to move 10 km. The Minister for Planning and Development, Mr. Hudson, could not say last week how much money had been spent on the trail.

No specific sum could be given because the work had been done by so many departments, including Planning and Development and the National Parks and Wildlife Service, and a lot of assistance had been received from walking clubs and private enthusiasts.

Officially, one man has been working on the physical construction of the Heysen Trail. He is a ranger of the NPWLS, Mr. David Schmidt.

Unsure

Others directly involved are a planning officer of the State Planning office, Mr. Hague Showell, and the officer in charge of field operations with the NPWLS, Mr. Ross Gobby.

They have done a remarkable job of planning and organisation, producing their own specifications for walking trails and a report on a survey of

by
WILLIAM RESCHKE

cent. of walkers least preferred a simple spine trail such as the proposed Heysen Trail.

But it indicated, too, the **difficulties of building a trail for walkers and riders.**

Strongest agreement between the two groups was in the need for excluding all trail bikes and vehicles.

Of the horse riders, 80 per cent. were prepared to share the track with

walkers, but on the other hand only 58 per cent. of the walkers were ready to share it with horses.

They pointed to erosion of sloping ground, fouling of water supplies, attraction of flies to droppings and a greater effect on the landscape through need for a larger trail.

Walkers also raised the point that if the spine was designed for horses as well as walkers, it would be necessary to take it over less steep and rugged country.

●Cont. Page 128

Knobs & Knockers for every door
69 The Parade Norwood Ph 42 1241

An article in The Advertiser suggesting it will take till the year 2376 to finish the Trail. We thrived on such challenges.

watch, no farewell party at the board. They just crossed his number off the list. Anyway my point is that we were not given much information about what was going on, so I can only tell you the little that was fed to me, and that only as it effects the story of the Heysen Trail.

About 1977 it appeared that some doubts about the efficiency of the State Planning Authority were being expressed by some Members of Parliament. During that year a report into the functions of the authority was commissioned from the Pac Poy Company. It was the results of this report or the small bits of it that I heard, that was to seal the fate of the Heysen Trail.

On one rare occasion I went into the office early one morning and this time I was summoned to Jim Daly's office where he told me not to leave the building as the Minister wanted to see us, a cold chill ran up and down my ample frame, I gulped a couple of times and began to search my brain for some infraction I might have committed and thereby prepare some form of defense. There were too many, anyway too late, we were on our way to the hallowed ground and soon found ourselves in the presence of Tom Casey Minister of Agriculture and Minister for Tourism Recreation and Sport. We shook hands, were introduced by Casey's minder, a most unlikely looking cove, he seemed tired and looked definitely ill. He showed no great joy at this event. Tom Casey was quite different, he was a farmer with land near Peterborough in the mid north, unusual for a Labor Member of Parliament. It is 20 years since that meeting but I can still see it in my mind very clearly. Casey was a little shorter than me with dark greying hair, broad shoulders, a well made neatly turned out man with a natural if somewhat transitory charm.

The message to us was simple. The Pac Poy report had recommended that the work of the State Planning Authority could be better done by the National Parks and Wildlife Service with the exception of the responsibility for the Long Distance Trails Committee, which in truth meant the Heysen Trail. This was to be handed over to the Dept. of Tourism, Recreation and Sport. Great news. Not so. Tom was a farmer not a walker, and he stated his position clearly; the Heysen Trail had been going nowhere for the last 9 years which was not surprising. What landowners would ever want the public tramping over their paddocks? His preferred option was to "get it out of the pigeon hole and bury it once and for all."

The fate of the Heysen Trail hung in the balance. "But Minister" said I, "The Heysen Trail is enormously popular. Even though there's not much of it, we are constantly getting a very high rate of inquiries. We get more questions about walking than any other activity." Tom Casey was still only slightly impressed. He once more expressed his concern regarding getting landowners to agree. I explained, I believed there was enough Crown

A huge line carved on an early map worried many a landowner and a bush-walker strides puposefully across an early publication

Land to do most of it without going on freehold property. Both Casey and the motley looking minder stared back unconvinced, I lowered my head onto the block. "Minister I assure you that I can build a pilot trail between Mt Magnificent and Mt Lofty of about 50km and complete it inside 3 months." Impressive stuff so I thought but Casey remained unmoved and the minder goggled back. It was Jim Daly who saved the day and probably the Heysen Trail. "Minister", he said, "think of the kudos that would accrue to you if you could show that your predecessor got 9km of trail completed in as many years then you take over and complete 50km in 3 months." "How much do you need" the question came without hesitation "10 grand." I answered without any thought. "OK" said Tom "get the paper work ready." It was over, we were outside the door and the Heysen Trail was well on its way.

The concept of the Heysen Trail was introduced to the public early in 1970. This was done in part at least via a brochure produced by the South Australian State Planning authority and introduced in these terms; 'A WALKING AND HORSE RIDING TRAIL IS TO BE ESTABLISHED FROM CAPE JERVIS TO THE NORTHERN FLINDERS RANGES. A DISTANCE OF 800KM. THE STATE PLANNING AUTHORITY IS RESPONSIBLE FOR SECURING THE ROUTE PROPOSED'. The front cover of the brochure had a photograph of a young man heavily booted and carrying a massive backpack striding over steep tortuous country with apparent ease. The publication went on to describe the route to be taken and some of the difficulties of securing the route were discussed. It also gave examples of overseas developments. It was a useful piece of work, but it had a major flaw, one that was going to make life hard for those who had to make the Trail, as opposed to writing about it.

Before any consultation had taken place a written description of the Trail was made public, but it was worse. On the back of the pamphlet was a map showing the route from Cape Jervis to Mt Babbage, not so bad in itself, except that the Heysen Trail was marked with a broad brush stroke. From the map the path looked to be 10 times wider than the nearby River Murray and about one fifth the width of the City of Adelaide, and gave the appearance of being several kilometres wide. When the publication found its way into the bush there were stirrings from Strathalbyn to Blinman, and some sharp words were spoken. The perception of the Heysen Trail as opposed to the reality was born and it was a perception that was to dog me for many years to come.

The pundits, the soothsayers and the fortune tellers came quickly to the fore; they gazed into the heavens, cast the runes and read the tarot cards. They predicted failure for the Trail, doom for all those associated with it. The Trail would change the way of life in the bush for ever. Pandora's Box would be opened the Gordian Knot cut. Each weekend there would arise from the city a great phalanx of bush walkers bearded and booted, who would strike out on the Heysen Trail to re-enact Napoleon's retreat from Moscow or Sherman's march to the sea. Boots striking firelight from the flintstones at every single stride. They would fill their backpacks with prime cattle their pockets with fat lambs, rupture water pipes and empty tanks, then at the end of the day they would cast themselves, lemming-like, down the nearest mineshaft or over a convenient cliff, in doing so ensuring their relatives an income for life from the subsequent 3rd party claim against the landowner. The publication was released in November of 1971, again a year later, and finally in 1976. By this time there were many copies in the bush and although little was said landowners north and south of the city waited for something to happen before they made their move.

The Heysen Trail may have sent a shiver of concern through the collective spines of the rural community but it had quite the reverse effect in other areas of the community. The fact that the initial proposal came form Warren Bonython gave the whole thing a great degree of credibility. The fact that it was then supported by a Liberal Minister Murray Hill and continued to be endorsed by the next ruling Labor Government ensured that the Heysen Trail would have a high profile in the State Parliament and appear often in the annals of Hansard.

In the years between 1978 and 1995 the Heysen Trail was to become more than a walking trail. Out of the concept came University Spring study camps, radio series, National television coverage both ABC and commercial, a community support group with 1000 members, two guide books and numerous wireless broadcasts, maps, guides, pamphlets and a whole series of secondary school activities involving students. In 1986 to celebrate the State's Jubilee year we had a Hans Heysen art show opened by Queen Elizabeth II.

In between these two extremes sat myself with the job of pleasing both sides. I have spoken to other trailmakers around the world and many of them have had the same feelings. It's lonely at the sharp end.

Securing the Route

I doubt that it would have been possible to create the Heysen Trail if we had not been left with a legacy of hundreds of miles of unmade roads. These reserves were almost unknown to the mass of South Australians until the NFC began to develop its network of paths through the Mt Lofty Ranges in 1969. Even then it took us a long time to realise just what we had found, and that realisation only came very slowly and it was many months before we came to understand the extent of the resource we had uncovered. We went through some very odd arguments with landowners and district councils who quite clearly did not want us to understand the true situation. Such a central role did those reserves play in the development of trails in South Australia that I think it is worth spending some time on them.

Our system of road reserves comes down the years directly from British Colonial rule. A very curious thing when you think about it. The Poms up to that time had no experience of planning a road system, in fact they had no roads worth the name since the Romans left some years ago. In fact it was quicker to get from London to Constantinople in 300AD than it was in 1850AD. In truth the English had little reason to build any major roads, living on a small Island with a long coastline and with numerous navigable rivers cutting deep into the land and blessed with a tidal range that could carry merchant shipping from one remote corner of the country to another at little expense. There had been no great incentive for a road system. In fact the first use of the word 'road' refers to a body of water and not land. South Australia presented a different set of problems. The settlers did of course take full advantage of the SA coastline hence the mosquito fleet of ketches and the development of the River Murray as a major shipway but this still left vast areas of land unconnected with ports, coast and rivers. They set out to develop a road network. It was to good old Colonel William Light that the job of surveying the colony was given, when in 1836 he became the Surveyor General of the colony and amongst other things was responsible for the survey of a system of roads or at least to reserve the land on which a system could be based. So the Colonel's men set forth into what must have been for them a formidable and forbidding country. All this took place long before the rural lands were taken up. The surveyors were Europeans and undertook the task with European populations in mind, as a consequence they often provided far more reserves than were strictly needed, and as the rural blocks were taken up many of the reserves were simply fenced in with the properties. Although the reserves would continue to show on title deeds many

The Bluff and Kings Head from the Heysen Trail

land managers chose to forget their existence. The legislation governing the old roads has evolved over the years and now rests within the Roads (Opening and Closing) Act 1932 with a number of procedural amendments. The fee simple, that is the actual control over the road is vested in the District Council up to the point where the sale to an adjoining owner must be approved by the Minister of Lands. The numbers and importance of reserves varies from area to area. However we always seemed to find sufficient unmade roads for our purposes. Not that we always wanted to use a road reserve and often the landowner with whom we were negotiating had problems with us locating a path on a reserve that ran through his property but it did provide me with a negotiating tool. Road reserves were very difficult to identify up until the 80's. The only record of the roads was made on title deeds and the old Hundred Plans kept by the Lands Dept. which at a scale of 1 inch to 80 chains and only showing the division of land with section numbers and few other features did not help much. The road reserves showed as an empty space between properties and although this was obviously a road the viewer had no indication as to whether the reserve was made or not. During the early 1980s the S.A. Lands Dept. began to produce a series of 1:50,000 topographic maps with an over print of property boundaries shown in purple. This made the study of road reserves much simpler and it was now a very easy thing not only to identify the reserves, but also to see if they had been developed, and by studying the contours, vegetation and creek systems make a reasonable judgment about their recreation value. So at last we had a fairly quick method of assessing the worth of a reserve. However this did not help when it came to Identifying the reserves on the ground The real problem was that most of the reserves were over 100 years old and the fences even if they had ever existed were not well maintained. There was often little incentive for the adjoining landowner to do so although the Roads Opening and Closing Act required the adjoining landowner to do this. A one chain road passing along the boundary of a paddock for, say a kilometre can provide a nice piece of free grazing but only if it is unfenced, so why carry out expensive maintenance which will be to the advantage of no one. The problem for us was how were we going to reestablish a right of way for walkers without the enormous expense of surveying each one? Added to this was the ingenuity of farmers and graziers, for what we now knew they had known for many a long year and had plenty of time to develop a range of strategies to forestall us.

*L*andowners often took an annual license on an adjoining road reserve from the District Council; this license however was only a license for a specific purpose, that was usually for grazing but could be for a variety of other uses. Whatever the license was for, it in no way extinguished the public right of way. Many landowners claimed to me that they had a lease on the road and therefore it was closed to the community where in fact they had an annual licence and the

right of way was intact. The problem was that many farmers believed this self created myth. I had some very unpleasant times being fronted by large angry red faced farmers who demanded to know "what the hell do you think you're doing" to which my standard reply was "I think I'm standing here and you're shouting at me. What the hell do you think you're doing?" This rarely had a calming effect on the situation but it made me feel a lot better I can tell you. I made it a policy to approach adjoining landowners first by either phone or letter

A sign designed to intimidate

whenever possible. Landowners also adopted other means of concealing the whereabouts of roads. One of the oldest means of disguising a reserve is to make it look as much like a private entrance as possible. I have seen elaborate gateways with stone pillars, wrought iron gates and cattle grids, to quite simple archways made from pine posts. Then there is the old trick of erecting a large aggressive warning sign – 'PRIVATE PROPERTY-KEEP OUT' – this sign always faces into the road reserve but will in fact be on a post just outside of the reserve placed there to intimidate walkers. Another old country ruse is to lock the gate on a public reserve with a padlock and chain which is of course quite illegal but always ignored by the authorities. This however can provide a good clue to the fact that it is public property. If more than one land owner wants to use an old road they will cut the chain and put in their own locks. To cover their backs the District Council will also put in their own lock, the fire service, ETSA and Telecom often do the same thing, so you can end up with more locks than chain, the sort of thing that Marley's ghost would have been proud to wear at Christmastide. We did not object to these ploys being used as long as the owner and the council were up front with us and admitted that the reserve was public property and did not object to walkers using them, after all we were just as keen to keep out off road vehicles as they were. We got to know most of the tricks in the road reserve game. Even so, few landowners would volunteer the whereabouts of a reserve and so the onus was clearly with us to prove the case and if we had to do it by paying the cost of a survey the Heysen Trail would never be finished. We slowly came to realize that no matter how old and unfenced a reserve might be there were less expensive ways of confirming its position.

Road reserves, no matter what their condition do not exist in isolation and at some point they must connect with a road that was clearly identified by its attendant fence lines, and so it proved. When seeking out a road that we were interested in, we often followed a gravel road and then a station track to a point where the reserve that we were looking for took off marked only by a single fence line or in some cases no fence at all. The best outcome for us was to have a double fence line one chain apart with no development in between. This being the best option it rarely occurred. Mostly what we found was a single fence, the dilemma for us was to decide on which side the public land was situated. Using the nearest double fence line as a bench mark we then, with compass and a decent pair of binoculars would back track across country until we could establish the position of the reserve in relation to the single fence. In fact it was not usually that difficult once we knew how to read the signs. Then it was quite easy to establish the position of a reserve particularly if it connected with a double fenced reserve at an obvious corner, cross road or junction. It was where the unmade reserve went off from a straight track even if there was a single fence line we had to establish on which side was the public land. Even in this situation we got some clues; on occasions we found the remains of well rotted post lying in the grass or grubbed up into a heap or the remains of old soft iron fencing wire, this was enough to give us vital clues.

Often we found that a single fence line would track across country denoting, say the western side of a road reserve, then would without a reason take a 90 degree turn, then continue on the eastern side of the reserve. On other occasions we found a paddock had been worked up into a fine tilth and where the road was, a one chain gap of uncultivated earth was left and then continued as a ploughed land clearly identifying our reserve. You will often see a chain wide band of trees and other vegetation cutting across country for no apparent reason, this on closer examination will usually turn out to be a road reserve.

Our policy on road reserves was defined, where a reserve was fenced on both sides we would deal only with the District Council, where the reserve was unfenced we would negotiate with both the District Council and the owners on the unfenced side or sides.

The Heysen Trail is a massive development, but it was not the obvious tasks, like clearing scrub in winter's rain, the backpacking of waymarkers up hill and down dale in February's heat or digging post holes in iron hard ground that was the most difficult part of the job. There were worse things, much, much worse and one of those was the rural public meeting. These meetings struck terror deep into my heart, it was a burden that I was to carry alone for the whole 15 years of the trails development.

When I nod my head, hit it please

I have been in my chequered career a mountaineer, rock climbing instructor, a whitewater canoeing coach and served my time on the Mendip Cave Rescue Team. Plenty of opportunity to become familiar with fear's cold-hand. However nothing had prepared me for the rigours of country South Australia and especially not country South Australia when roused.

In truth meetings of landowners varied greatly, some were even quite gentlemanly and productive and on rare occasions even good humoured but it is the bad ones that I remember.

I always knew that it would be bad tactics to meet farmers collectively and this I avoided wherever possible, but the man and woman on the land are astute, and most have a good measure of natural cunning; whereas my strategy was to divide and conquer, theirs was never to divide their forces in the face of the enemy and so it usually came about that a public meeting was called.

I shall not try to describe each of the meetings I attended but provide this composite picture instead.

Public meetings always seemed to be held on Friday nights, during winter, dark, cold and wet. Although the route of the Trail in a particular district would usually only affect 10 or 12 landowners these meetings often attracted 40 or more locals.

For the first time ever a public servant was to be on show and put to the test and so all the landowners from the properties near and far would gather to see the fun.

The venue would be the Soldiers Memorial Hall or the Mechanics Institute. This cavernous building would have been built in the mid 1930s and had only been used twice since, once for a wedding and in more recent times to celebrate the Queen's Coronation, Elizabeth II that is. The building itself was substantial, of generous proportions cold and damp with small windows and high ceiling, painted overall in a chalky white covering that seemed to have little adhesion to its host walls and ceiling. The floor was of good quality wood but it had long ago given up its once lustrous sheen and was now a light grey, beginning to curl at the edges and although recently swept, gave off an odour like a gymnasium just after the combatants had left.

Let battle commence:

From all around the district farmers were finishing their dinners of woodstove lamb and climbing into an assortment of utes and 4 wheel drive vehicles and heading into town. Meanwhile I was parked in some off road piece of scrub where I had been, fearing lateness for the last hour, suffering the agonies of anticipation. So I arrived in town, the meagre street lighting reflecting back from bitumen and sodden blue stone kerbing. I angle parked in the main street, still harbouring hopes that (a) I had got the wrong night, (b) nobody would turn up or (c) a virulent plague had swept through the district; but the main street was full, there are more vehicles parked in the street tonight than I have seen here before. The building filled.

A battered ute pulled in beside me, the obligatory Blue Heeler guarding the tray top, he crossed to my side registering his contempt for me. Even the dogs are against me! His owner walked around to me, a friendly looking sort, "Youse' the bloke from the Government? "he speculates." "Yes" I confessed. His mahogany face split beneath the aged Akubra, "Jesus mate you're going to have an 'orrible night", he predicted with glee and passed into the Institute determined to get a good seat.

The odds were forty to one that I was about to get a mauling. It was 7.30 on a Friday night, most of my colleagues, the Director, the CEO all the bright young things, the coming men, those with great expectations, were safe, warm and dry in or on their way to homes, pubs, discos, and small warm steamy restaurants. Only the common foot soldier was on duty. The Chairman called the meeting to order, they do as they're asked. He apologised for the District Clerk who had fled, pleading variously, a wedding, funeral, or bar mitzvah and was on his way to Adelaide, lucky bastard.

The Chairman outlined the rules of the engagement. He said he understood the emotions of the issue and directed that I should be treated as a guest, it was a nice gesture but the fact that he had to say it provided me with no comfort at all. I was about to be asked to address the gathering. I was not blessed with any natural talent, no skill or artistic bent but as I have matured the features of my face have set, they have become rather satisfyingly grim. I am never asked for donations in the street, religious callers rarely linger at our door and even quite large dogs have been known to detour around me. Also this face shows no fear regardless of the state of my nerves. It was now that I could bring this talent to bear, as far as the meeting would ever know I was supremely confident, assured of success and not in any way intimidated by the hostility that I was facing.

I got the hammering I expected of course, but had they even sensed the doubt it would have been a rout. As it was, a bit more understanding had developed amongst the landowners, a slight change, a softening towards the Trail. As I fielded the major questions, fire risk, third party liability, fences, gates, litter, funding future maintenance costs, I felt the more reasonable landowners relaxing a little. The more radical elements also feeling the initiative slipping away from them, they began to ask a series of irrelevant and hypothetical questions, native title, spread of rye grass toxicity, loss of superphosphate bounty. This only served to isolate them further.

The meeting would begin to flag at about this time, the same questions being repeated and as pub closing time was drawing near, the Chairman had no difficulty in bringing the meeting to an end and we would then tramp into the still wet street. I often arranged to stay at the pub overnight but just as often could not face another round of hostility in the bar, and so climbed into my trusty Landcruiser to drive the 200 miles through the night. Just one of the many lonely journeys I would make over the next 15 years

The private land managers, lease holders, and owners were far too numerous to list here, although many are mentioned elsewhere. We met some of the biggest pastoral companies in the country, including the Kidman Company which I thought very fine indeed as I was reading Ion Idriess' book "Cattle King" at the time. I also met many farmers of more modest status. We had some tough times together battling out the route of the Trail but there was some fun and games too.

During the planning of the Trail I had contact with over 600 land managers either the landowners themselves or their agents whose land adjoined the proposed trail. There were also pastoral and perpetual lease holders, 18 State Government Departments, even a couple of Federal Agencies, and just to complicate things further, 26 District Councils. Their owners ranged over the whole gambit of rural industries, pine plantations, viticulture, gold mining, rehabilitation of alcoholics, wheat growing, quarrying, beef and dairy cattle, tourism, vegetables and fruits, sheep and goats, and I even got mixed up with ferrets and llamas at one stage.

The Government Departments were as you might expect National Parks and Wild Life Service, Woods and Forests, Dept. of Lands, Government Printer, Premiers Dept., SA Police, Education Dept. Agriculture Dept., E&WS, South, Australian Tourism Commission, Civil Aviation Authority, Dept. of Territories, Mines and Energy, Health Dept., Commonwealth Employment Service, Pastoral Board, Treasury, Crown Solicitor,. Highways Dept. and the State Transport Authority.

I met some splendid farmers going through the process, we got

Walkers enjoying the fruits of our labours

some good work done, had some laughs and added to our ever growing knowledge on the art of trail making.

Approaching landowners on the delicate subject of public access to their properties, was never going to be easy and I had to choose my time carefully – no good for instance trying during a drought. Just after a decent rain was good but you had to get in quick before seeding started. Nobody wanted to know me during harvest, crutching or shearing. Then there was milking morning and night, grape picking and vintage. Friday is shopping day in the bush and it's bowls on Saturday and of course everybody goes to the tennis in Adelaide at least once a year. What with field days the Adelaide Show and the butchers' picnic I was lucky to ever get to see anyone.

Negotiating rights of way was not a skill that you could buy a book about or get on a training course, God knows why not, though there were courses on just about everything else!. So we had to develop our own tactics. Here are some of the basic ground rules that we devised. I discovered, never visit a landowner during a drought, or seeding nor on Friday which is as I said before is shopping day in the bush. Even if you never wear a hat, get one, put it on just before you knock on the farmhouse door. If the wife answers whip it smartly from your head, this really impresses the ladies of the bush, always try to do the deal with the son; they are a lot more understanding than the old man. Don't talk to farm dogs, don't pet or stroke them. This is considered the same as talking to a broom or a chainsaw or any other tools. Try to find out the difference between a cyclone fence and a bag of super. Above all try to avoid discussing rights of way when the wife is present. No, don't get me wrong. I have developed the greatest respect for the woman on the land, it is that they are much better negotiators than the men and will always get the better deal! Don't call a cocky 'sir' or 'mate' , first names are the usual form of address in the country. Always shake hands, but be prepared to suffer some degree of pain of which you must not show any sign. All farmers have strong hands regardless of age, this comes from a lifetime of shearing , crutching, fencing and depriving sheep and cattle and other beasts of their various body parts. Remember if you have to visit some far flung part of a property a cocky will not walk, do not offer to take him in your vehicle however, the cocky will always want to drive, go in his wagon. When being driven by a cocky it is essential that you show no fear, whether you are driving up the steepest of ridges or plunging down into a gully, do not hang on to the dashboard or brace your feet against the floor – this will betray you as a city dweller. As the front seat passenger, tradition decrees that it is your task to open the gates. In so doing, leave the vehicle smartly, preferably while it is still moving, this always impresses land owners. If you are unfamiliar with farm gates then you are in deep trouble. Farm gates are a complex series of devices, no two are the

26

same and they take a lifetime of experience and the ability of a master safe breaker to have an understanding of the way in which they work or more correctly, they don't work. The only way to overcome this deficiency is to practice secretly and the time spent will be well worth it. Nothing is more demeaning in the bush than having leapt from a fast moving ute to be faced with a mass of old rusty wire a variety of bent star droppers, and the inevitable four or five hundred yards of black bailing string and being unable to master its complexities, then having to return shame faced to the wagon and to ask the cocky for help.

Some of the meetings that I had are particularly memorable. Part of the third section of the Trail had to connect land to the north and south of the Yulte Conservation Park taking in a goat breeder and two dairy farms. The Trail came from the south out of a property and into a well timbered and rutted lane, a road reserve with the fences intact on both sides. Just as the lane turned steeply up a sharp stony pinch into the park it passed a small neat house, the home of Mr and Mrs Bayment. When we were passing the Bayment home on a trail assessment, the owner came out and asked us what we were up to. Imagine our surprise to find ourselves being addressed in a broad rich brogue straight out of Thomas Hardy's Dorset - right there in a remote Gully in South Australia. The next landowner on the north of the conservation park was Mr Radnotti, an Italian gent with only a modest command of the English language. After some time spent showing him maps, plans and letters with a fair amount of pantomime thrown in, with no apparent progress being made, I came to the conclusion that Mr Radnotti had built his small dairy over part of the road reserve. After this was pointed out we got along much faster and were able to put the Trail on a more suitable part of the property.

On to the next land holding, another dairy but owned by Australian, Mr Brian Brown. Brian's country occupied part of the valley between Mt Myponga and the Myponga reservoir. We met and I explained the general outline of the scheme to which Brian gave his approval. But when we got to the details his demeanour changed, title deeds were brought out, mouths began to set. "This so-called road of yours passes right through my best pasture. I can't have walkers disturbing our stock at all hours of the day and night." I must have looked somewhat crestfallen. "Look mate you see that ridge up there, could you take the Trail over that?". He pointed east towards a splendid rocky ridge running north to south. "Well", says I, "we might at that, can we go and have a look?" "Yes", said Brian considerably cheered, "but I'm not bloody well walking up there, we'll take the tractor."

Well as everyone knows, tractors are only made for one and as it was Brian's machine he got to drive, with me standing on a sort of tow bar at the back of the vehicle, gripping the left-hand giant rear mudguard my only hand hold. Brian gave me a briefing. "If she goes over when we are going up hill jump sideways; if it happens on the way down just step off the back."

We began our ascent of the ridge. As it happened it was not the steepness of the rise that made the journey memorable, but quite another hazard. As we crossed the rich verdant pasture we came into contact with the cow droppings; fresh, semi liquid, sweet and strong smelling. I am from the country, the English country it is true, but a cow is a cow after all. Seen from 6 feet above on the back of a tractor, a cow pat or two is nothing, but as we climbed on I found that the tractor's great driving wheels would pass through a clump of the stuff. As I watched with disgust, it adhered to the deep tread of the tyre and came up inch by inch to where my hands clutched the mud guard and then liberally coated them with a thick layer of the still warm manure.

This happened afresh every few minutes. When Brian saw what was happening he thoroughly enjoyed my discomfort, calling back to me "I keep telling them not to do that but they won't listen." Another fine addition to the Trail was made that afternoon but at what cost?

Mt Magnificent to Mt Lofty

We never did get the cash that Tom Casey promised. This made life difficult. I had promised the Minister that I would prove all the opponents of the Trail wrong by creating a 50km pilot trail without difficulties in less than 3 months. Due to my years wandering in the wilderness, well the Mt Lofties anyway, I had the route of the path fairly well defined in my mind and had sounded out many of the land managers (not that I had told the Dept. it was essential to the scheme of things that they believed I was starting from scratch).

We made an application to the department of Aboriginal affairs who were offering funding for a training program for young Aboriginal men. Once again we were successful and received funding to employ four men plus funding for tools, equipment and the all important 4-WD truck

The new staff in addition to Richard and myself, was Black Bob, Hippo, Big Norman and Lionel, via the Dept. of Aboriginal Affairs and Martin Augustin, a Sweetpea (SYETP)

With this unlikely but happy band, we set off into the Mt Lofties to write ourselves into the history books. Working with Aboriginal men for the first time was quite an experience.

This pilot section of the Trail was far more important than anyone, even the clever buggers in the office, could know. It was this development that would make or break the project. We would be forced into some real issues. Funding, manpower, liaison with other Government Departments, use of freehold land, use of unmade road reserves, camping, promotion and publicity, design of facilties, purchasing of materials and manufacture of signs and way markers.

As far as the making of things I could leave that in the hands of Richard. We had enough funds to buy timber and a few basic tools but not much else. So the success of the whole manufacturing side of things was solely reliant on the staff's initiative and inventive genius, and it never failed, well almost never.

Black Bob was a timber cutter from NSW and could do some remarkable things with a chainsaw. In fact, so beloved was he of this deadly tool that once he got hold of one it was difficult to get him to put it down. I am still surprised that we all ended the year with the required number of limbs and other appendages. That is to say, all except Martin who did, but only after some quick thinking by Black Bob and some nimble micro-surgery at the Royal Adelaide.

The Farmer and Stock Owner, Feb 1984.

The worst aspect of the Heysen Trail is that the landowners who will be affected by its establishment and who 'know' the type of land it will be crossing were not consulted by the Government...and still have not been consulted on where the Trail should go.

This according to property owners near Wirrabara, David Blesing and Peter Pole has the Trail proposal a 'ridiculous' one.

" It was only recently that we were told of the planned trail and since then have seen 2 paths for it to take ," they said.

In some places , the Trail follows old surveyed roads which are now obsolete and in other parts , people would be expected to walk over cliffs.

For one of our neighbours, the Trail would mean a complete lack of privacy as it is proposed to pass between his house and sheds," Peter Pole said. "no one should have to accept that

"A suggestion might be to keep the Trail right away from houses and roads but then there would be the problem of people walking through mostly inaccessible and dangerous country.

The cost of replacing property ruined by vandals could also run into hundreds or thousands of dollars.

Even without the extra tourists attracted by the Trail, the landowners in the area have had to put up new fences and gates, driven over because people were too lazy to open them, and replace wrecked windmills and stock killed just for the hell of it."

Carolyn Miller Feb 1984.

In Richard Massey we had a true inventive genius; conventional signwriting was expensive, and unsuitable due to the high maintenance costs. What we needed and what proved to be so effective was wooden routed signs, but we could not afford a router. Richard acquired a second hand electric drill from somewhere and with a few pieces of scrap galvanized fencing iron produced an oddly efficient machine. We could now make our own waymarkers. and it was not long before we were able to produce complete warning and information signs carved into wooden planks of any size.

This development was also born of Massey's fertile brain. It was a device that consisted of a series of steel strips loosely bolted together in a fashion that resembled a piece of trellis fencing. It worked in this way, the router was bolted at one end and at the other was fixed a pointer. When this pointer was made to follow a particular shape, say in our case a letter in a book, the router if started and placed in position on a piece of wood now carved the original letter into the wood. By moving the pointer the router could be persuaded to reproduce the original shape but at varying sizes.

Oh dear, oh dear what would today's 'We are not hands on' public servants make of all this? Richard invented a series of gadgets which if not for the benefit of mankind certainly made life easier for us. He went on to design the self clamping routing bench, a photo light sensitive box for the making of silk screens, a geodesic dome green house to name but a few.

However his solar kettle was less successful, and his attempt to convert an abandoned caterpillar tractor into a mechanical post hole digger, was nearly fatal.

While the workshop was being organised I set out to define the route and began to contact the landowners. The chosen route of the Trail was from the summit of Mt Magnificent, through the Mt Magnificent Conservation Park, along Black Fellows Creek, through The Central Methodist Church land at Kuitpo Colony, into the Kyeema Conservation Park, then through the Kuitpo and Knots Hill Forest, over Dashwood Gully Road, into the Mt Bold Reservoir Reserve, over the Jupiter Creek Goldfields, along Bradys Gully, over the Onkaparinga River, through the Mylor Rec. Reserve and the Englebrecht National Trust Land and Stirling DC reserve along Cox Creek.

It then traversed the Education Dept.'s Arbury Park Land, across a reserve dividing the Mt Lofty Golf Club and finally in to Cleland Conservation Park and on to the summit of Mt Lofty. These properties were all joined together by a series of unmade or under-developed Road Reserves. So I sallied forth to begin to negotiate a right of way with the various landowners.

My first port of call was to be the Kuitpo Colony, an isolated settlement some 40km south of Meadows in the valley of Black Fellows Creek. At the time the Colony was run as a treatment and rehabilitation centre for alcoholics. When I told my wife what my next day's work was to be, she became agitated, she was concerned that once in such a place I might find it difficult to persuade the management to let me leave.

I entered the Colony with mixed feelings, this was something entirely new to me. Not to worry, I was given a hearty welcome by the management, then introduced to the farm manager who offered to give me the grand tour before joining the inmates for lunch. I don't exactly know what I expected to find during the tour, screams, wild moaning, the clank of chains perhaps. There was of course nothing like this. What I did meet was a number of quite ordinary men doing an assortment of interesting things in a workshop, some with great skill, and later went to the cattle yards to watch another group of men doing things to some of the biggest bulls I have ever seen. Just what they were up to I am still unsure although it was carefully explained to me at the time and I know it caused me to suck the air in over my teeth. The blokes got right in amongst the cattle and there was a good deal of unpleasantness. I thought that they showed considerable courage. The deal was done over lunch and I was able to select the route.

During the next few days I set out on a long round of calls to Parks and Wildlife Service and Woods and Forest Head offices, then the respective regional offices to meet the managers on the ground. At this time I also wrote to the E&WS seeking permission to cross the Mt Bold Reservoir. Everything went well with 'Parks', as it did with the 'Forests', everyone involved being enthusiastic about the project. There were conflicts of course but we were soon able to sort them out. The SA Police had some questions regarding the Echunga training camp and their horse breeding stud just to the north of the Jupiter Gold Field but were soon onside. The National Trust gave their permission to use Engelbrecht Reserve. The Stirling District Council were more than helpful with general information and names of landowners and addresses. We were soon through to Arbury Park and the Education Dept. who after reasonable debate gave their whole-hearted support to the Trail.

The way was almost clear to Mt Lofty, then the crunch came. I went to Bolivar at the request of the E&WS to see the Chief Chemist, who was not available when I arrived. However the Heysen Trail file was found after some time and passed over to me. Written across its benign buff cover in large bold red letters was the uncompromising message – 'NO WAY.'

This was a major setback, but later I realized that I had been talking to a scientific officer, an industrial chemist in fact, who saw things from a very narrow perspective.

I resolved to go through the negotiating process again, guiding the application to the head office in Victoria Square where the application got a better reception. Their agreement for the Trail to cross the headwaters of Jupiter Creek was forthcoming, albeit with some modification and under strict conditions.

During the building of the Trail we did many more deals of this sort with the E&WS and they always worked well. The negotiations were now complete and the physical labor of making the Trail could begin in earnest. At the same time a map and brochure had to be produced, something that none of us knew much about.

The Mapping Division of the Lands Dept. produce one of the finest 1:50,000 topographic maps in the world. It was to them and to the Government Printer that I took my problem, and

Cover of Section 6 of the Heysen Trail mapsl

received far more help than I could reasonably have expected. They took portions of the Onkaparinga, Noarlunga and Echunga maps and put them together into a strip map.

I now met Oli Laukirbe at the Premier's Department who was responsible for a variety of State publications. His first reaction to my proposal was that I should stop annoying people in general and him in particular with grandiose schemes that would never work. With the help of the departments we were able to put together a very credible publication, one that set the pattern for the other 14 Heysen Trail Maps. More of maps later.

We had some more fun building a bridge over Cox Creek at Arbury Park. None of us had any experience with building bridges, except Martin Augustin who had seen a film called 'Bridge over the River Kwai' and he took on the role of consulting engineer.

We were almost bereft of funds by the time it came to build the bridge and we were forced to scrounge the materials. We ended up with an assortment of pine posts and a considerable quantity of fencing wire, and of course several miles of black baling string and this had to suffice.

The boys went at it with a will and soon had the creek spanned by logs and by the time I got back to check on progress they even had one handrail up on the left hand side. Cox Creek is not usually difficult to cross but does drain the eastern slopes of Mt Lofty and Mt Bonython and much of the Piccadilly Valley and so after rain it can be a very hazardous crossing. The very reason for us feeling it necessary to provide a bridge.

It was such a day as this when I arrived, the creek surging along all foam and back eddies. I was invited to be the first to use the structure. I stepped out smartly enough and was soon standing in the middle of the bridge where the long posts met. It was definitely unpleasant out there and as I turned to go back to the safety of the bank, the toe of my boot caught on a protruding bolt head causing me to stumble. I made a grab for the upstream handrail which alas had not yet been put in place, the bridge swayed down stream and I launched myself into the foaming torrent. Later some walkers who witnessed the feat told me that it was done with considerable aplomb, I was momentarily airborne and then the violent cataract closed about me and I was off towards Bridgewater at high speed.

If not for my training and skill as a whitewater canoeist (I usually have the advantage of a kayak) I am sure I would have finished the day in the Mt Bold Reservoir, but years of training stood me in good stead. I surfaced, neatly ferry glided across a vertical eddy and grabbed the trailing wands of a friendly willow.

I pulled myself into the shallows and to my feet then on to the bank, where I expected to find my loyal staff hurrying to the assistance of their amphibious leader. Not so, what I did find was my trusted band writhing about the river bank like an illustration from the Kama Sutra in uncontrollable hysterics. Isambard Kingdom Brunel you have nothing to fear.

The date for the official opening of the Trail was set for the 17th of November 1978 at the picnic ground in Arbury Park and we were now progressing steadily towards completion. It would be tight but I was confident we would make it, I had of course not reckoned with fate's contrary hand, in which was firmly grasped an adjustable spanner of the larger type, which was now cast with unerring aim deep into the works. We had used a long stretch of fire break in the Kuitpo forest, all well marked as required with pine waymarkers set deeply into hand dug post holes, a labour of love. Now it came to pass that this being early spring the break was due for its yearly slashing, done as on many occasions before, by a contractor who now proceeded to mow the break. When he came to our markers he steadfastly refused to cut around them, instead bulldozing them over with his tractor, something he apparently thoroughly enjoyed. "No one told me" was his only comment. With just 7 working days to go we now had 10 days work ahead of us and a team rapidly tiring from overlong days and a lot of hard physical work in cold wet conditions. But fate had not yet finished with us.

The maps were being prepared by the Lands Department mapping division, and were then to be printed by the Government Printer. The strip maps were made up from of parts of several 1:50,000 Topographic maps.

The Heysen Trail was drawn on transparent paper and would be used to print the route of the Trail over the finished map. We had already run into trouble with the costing and had to reluctantly produce the map in 4 colours not 6 which gave the thing a rather muddy appearance. The maps were ready 2 days before the opening, and I remember the anxious wait as we undid the first bundle and there was our map, not a bad looking piece of work considering, but wait a minute something did not seem quite right, at first nobody could see it, then the penny dropped, somehow the transparent overlay had been reversed then realigned by an unknown person not familiar with the Trail. The result of this was that the Trail started at the Mt Lofty summit alright but then slowly drifted away to the west as the Trail went south until by the time it reached the bottom end of the map instead of arriving at the summit of Mt Magnificent it was somewhere over Willunga Hill.

The boys at the printers were suitably contrite. The transparency was correctly aligned and they worked through the night to give us, in the nick of time, a map that we introduced to the public.

The great day arrived and beneath a clear blue spring sky Warren Bonython and Minister Tom Casey jointly opened the first 50km section. We shared a few hours of self congratulations, but by Monday morning I was on the move. Something about the Heysen Trail had caught the community's imagination.

All three television stations had sent crews along to the opening and that night we had great coverage. By the time I got into the office the next morning the calls for information, in far greater numbers than we had ever imagined, were rolling in. All the radio stations wanted to do phone interviews, Channel 9 Kids Show wanted a live segment and I even went on a day time television show called 'A Touch of Elegance'.

I have never considered myself to be particularly elegant nor has it ever been suggested that walkers or walking was a very elegant activity. It was a very odd experience. To see the set on a television screen you would have sworn that the show was being transmitted from some affluent lounge room somewhere in the Mt Lofty Ranges. It was all fake, some coloured photographs, a few bits of curtain, a lounge suite and a borrowed coffee table and the illusion was complete, but it was well done and it did provide us with an avenue to publicise the Trail. It seemed that everybody wanted to walk on the Heysen Trail, and suddenly we were flavour of the month. So it was that the Department now had something big and bold to hang its hat on and from this small start we were to go on to become one of the best known Government initiatives.

Not everyone was happy about this and over the next 10 years we were to find a small group of knockers would always be with us. The first of these struck during the week of the opening. It transpired that a group of walkers who were particularly proud of their level of fitness decided to seek fame and glory by being the first to complete the 50km of the Trail in a single day. This they failed to do, and put the blame on the marking of the Trail, but if the Trail itself was to blame, which it was later found not to be the case, the reasonable thing to do was to report the problem to the Department. The action these walkers took was to hawk the story around the newspapers. The News published their story in the Thursday evening edition. The next day I was called to the Minister's office to explain. It is often said that there is no justice in this world, well there is certainly none in the Public Service.

The brass hats are paid vast sums of money, which is in part to compensate them for 'carrying cans, and stopping bucks ' and all that garbage. In my experience they got the money and I carried a wide variety of bucks, tins, held the ends of effluent coated sticks, short straws, and frequently paid the piper. The worst aspect of this was that when I finally got to wear the brass hat they changed the rules and I became a frequent passenger in the tumbrel. The Public Service holds to a simple if unwritten rule. If an employee is accused of inefficiency, a breach of discipline, behaviour unbecoming, he is assumed to be guilty. The only consideration then is how to minimise the political damage to the Minister.

On this occasion there was a lot more to the story than emerged immediately. One of the walkers did phone me and apologise for all the trouble saying that it had all gone much too far. Since this time a much fuller picture of the incident has emerged. I have been told that the walkers had left their car at the summit of Mt Lofty with a note on the windscreen explaining that they would return later that day. On the same day that all this happened Black Bob and some of the other aboriginal blokes working on the Trail were approached by a group of walkers and they cajoled Bob in to giving them a lift in the Landcruiser down part of the Trail. Whether these were the same walkers that made the complaint I could never find out. Meanwhile back at the summit of Mt Lofty their car with its attendant note had attracted the attention of the police. It was the embarrassment of this that I believe was the cause of their 'oh so public' complaint. I had to explain to Casey and his minder what had happened. Some mindless reply was made in the press that week. What was really worrying about this affair was that it now seemed to me that Tom Casey was not a supporter of the Trail nor ever had been, he'd given the go ahead back in June in the certainty that the thing was not possible, and now despite the good press, this one setback had confirmed his negative view. There was no need to worry, there was now a cabinet shuffle and we became part of the newly formed Ministry of Community Development with John Bannon as Minister.

I was soon introduced to John by Tom Casey and during this intro-duction my views about Tom's lack of commitment to the Trail were confirmed, for as I stood facing them explaining what I did, Tom joined in and advised John Bannon not to have a bar of it, saying he did, and look where it led. But John Bannon made it very clear that he was a walker and thought it a splendid initiative.

So the year drew to an end, we had faced up to many of the prob-lems that dog trail makers, we had weathered some crises, copped some good and bad press, established a workshop, proved our ability to manufacture Trail furniture and now had a new young Minister who understood what we were about.

On the downside the Aboriginal funding was due to run out and with our labour force would go the 4-wheel drive which we had bought from part of the funding. The SYETP funding was also running out and there seemed every prospect that Richard Massey and myself might make up the trail's staff with only conventional vehicles at our disposal.

I have already told some of the story of the young Aborigines in a previous chapter and here is the rest of the story. I had seen the opportunity to get some funds for the Trail from The Department of Aboriginal Affairs and so put in my bid. I was soon advised against the application by several senior members of the department, trotting out the usual stereotypes of Aboriginal people. Predicting all kinds of trials and tribulations for me if I went ahead with the scheme.

I had by this time been in South Australia for almost 10 years. I hadn't in fact met any Aborigines. Although I was aware of the prejudice that seemed to be quite rampant in some parts of the community. Sadly it had been my experience that the more formal an education an Australian had and the more responsibility they held, the more prejudiced they could appear to be. The ordinary working person in factory or building site seems to handle mixed race situations far easier than those up the social scale. However I respected the Director's opinion enough to think long and hard about the applications and in the end decided to go ahead. I can't however claim some high motive. My project was going nowhere without staff and money. The application was accepted and so by March 1978 we had on the staff four Aboriginal men, some limited funds and a 4 wheel drive vehicle.

Throughout August and September the Trail progressed, the construction team working well, and the route was almost secure. I will always value the time I spent with the Aboriginal blokes.

Being an Englishman who did not arrive in Australia until I was 28 years of age, I'd had little contact with white Australians and none at all with Aborigines. Although I had throughout my life met and got on well with people of many races and of a wide range of skin colours, I'd even spent two years as a sales rep working in the East End of London. We seemed to mix in alright, a myriad of races and religions all with a single purpose, to make a decent living in the less than affluent Britain of the 1960s.

My only knowledge of Australia and of it's people was from half heard geography lessons, dog eared school text books left over from the grim depression days of the 1930s' and from films. Consequently it was my distinct impression that Australia was a large flat dusty plain, covered in empty beer cans and kangaroos and where all the inhabitants look like Chips Rafferty, even the women. The only reference to Aborigines was in a film I had seen called something like 'Smiley Gets A New Bike' during a brief scene where Smiley's father admonished him for going to the Black Fellows camp. So it was with some mixed feelings that I found myself managing a group of young black men.

Names can be all important to some people. I have never minded being called a 'Pommy' or 'Limey' in fact I could wear it with a bit of pride, and I've had French mates who didn't bat an eye at being 'Frogs', Italians who were 'Wops' and a boating mate who we never really knew his country of origin but was happy to answer to the name of 'Tony the Wog'. How would a group of Aborigines recently arrived in the city accept a white man, and an Englishman at that, as their manager?

I need not have concerned myself. The first few days sorted the thing out and put our relationship on a friendly workman like basis. I was the boss to be known as 'The Boss'. I was a white feller, Black Bob, Hippo, Big Norman, and Lionel, were black fellas.

It was quite an education working with them.

Black Bob was always at work on time. No matter how early I got there, Bob was waiting. One morning I had to take my wife Ann to catch the breakfast flight to Melbourne and in doing so passed the workshop. There sitting forlornly on the steps was Bob, it was 6:30am, at least an hour before starting time. Later that morning I asked Bob what he was up to "Well boss I don't like to be late for work but I don't use a clock or watch, so when the sun rises I go to work."

On another occasion Hippo did not turn up for work. We kept the truck waiting for an hour then sent them on their way. The next day Hippo explained that he had been sick and couldn't come to work. Fair enough, we all do it, however I emphasized the need to get in touch with Richard or me so as not to keep the vehicle and the other men waiting. Hippo understood. Some 3 weeks later I was awoken by an insistant telephone at 3am. It was Hippo advising of his inability to come to work later that day. Hoist by my own petard!

It was with great sadness that we said our farewells to Hippo, Black Bob, Lionel, Big Norman and Martin. We had had a roller coaster of a time together. An experience that I will always remember.

We waited for the Landcruiser to be withdrawn, in fact it never was, somehow it had been included in the Division's vehicle allocation and it was changed every 2 years for a new one from then on. We did not complain and the error was never discovered. It was one of the few things that remained constant.

Newlands Hill to Mt Magnificent

In June of that year the Heysen Trail was opened by Kym Mayes at a public picnic on the gum-treed slopes of Mt Magnificent, taking the length of the way to close to 200km, almost a long distance trail in itself.

The area between Mt Magnificent and the south coast was not well known to us.

Mt Magnificent is not a lofty mountain in the true sense of the word but it does have the form and shape of an alpine peak, steep sided with a long summit ridge leading up from the northern gullies. A

Majestic vistas to the South Coast abound

climb up its steep flanks on a warm clear winter's day to its summit will provide all the explanation of its name that is required.

I met two splendid characters when looking for a way to the south from Mt Magnificent. AC and DC Dash, were longtime dairy men who regarded me with deep suspicion, however I got on with them well enough in the end to be privileged to be shown their solar water heater that provided them with hot showers at the end of the day.

There was a reserve running south past their house which I finally got their blessing to use. Sadly they were burnt out during the fires of 1983 and I never saw them again.

There is a fine old cart or wagon track benched into a very steep hillside which leads down from the ridge through the Finnis Conservation Park and then follows the Finnis River, a great walk. To the south east of Mt Compass is the property of Willowburn through which there was some interesting country, all accessible via Crown Land and which would connect the Mt Compass Nangkita Road with the butter factory about 8km to the south.

I contacted the adjoining owner who turned out to be a member of the Upper House. The gentleman invited me to meet him on the property where he would show me a much better route for the Trail than the one that I was proposing. We duly met; he was full of enthusiasm for the Trail but when It came to his superior pathway it was all on roads and far from his Willowburn farm. I declined his offer and pointed to the greatly superior nature of my original route, this he accepted with good grace, if somewhat glumly. From Willowburn the way passes over Mt Cone a strenuous walk but worth it for views alone. From here you get your first glimpse of the Bluff and Victor Harbor to the south and if you then face the north Mt Lofty can still be seen.

My thoughts had already turned to the development of the Trail along the south coast of the Fleurieu Penninsula, that is to say connecting Cape Jervis with Newland Hill. Although I knew little about the area, having only been there with the Clayton Outward Bound School on some of their rock climbing exercises, I had seen enough to impress me with its spectacular cliffs and seascapes.

Cape Jervis to Newland Head

In 1980 the south coast was fairly remote and I decided that the only way to really asses its potential was to backpack along the cliff tops and foreshore with the object of staying within the coastal reserve, another valuable legacy from the far sighted Colonel Light whereby he had directed that there should be a reserve of 150 links from the high water mark for the 'recreation and education of the people of South Australia'. Ian Trestrail, another officer from the Dept. agreed to go with me if we could make suitable arrangements. As it turned out, it wasn't until March of the following year that we were able to get time to go.

The difficulty I had with this timing was that it had been a very dry summer, particularly so for the Fleurieu Peninsula, and although it was now late March the fire risk was still high and the water situation was doubtful. The thought of postponing the job was not an attractive one. Ian's commitments were quite heavy and although my work arrangements were more flexible it might be 6 months or more before we could get together again, and so we decided to go, carrying as much water as was feasible and live off cold rations. We did take a small spirit stove with us just in case the weather broke during the week. Not wishing to tie up a Government car and a driver we persuaded our wives Mary Trestrail and Ann Lavender to drop us off at Cape Jervis on the Sunday and pick us up in Victor Harbor a week later. So we arrived at the jetty on Cape Jervis at 3pm on a very warm day towards the end of March 1980. We made the final adjustments to our equipages made our fond farewells and strode manfully towards Victor. When we reached the low summit of a sand ridge I turned to make my final good bye wave which was returned. I turned my back on civilization and heard drifting faint on the soft sea breeze my wife's last farewell "Lavender you must be raving mad". She was as always correct.

We had an eventful journey along that spectacular coast. The first night spent in a shallow creek bed east of Fishery Beach near some fishing shacks.

Now things began in earnest. The second day started with some minor climbs over low ridges and headlands the way becoming more magnificent with every step. We passed into the Deep Creek Conservation Park and lunched at Blowhole Beach, where we were disappointed not to find water. The way now changed character, the creeks and gullies becoming deeper and steeper That afternoon was a continuous battle with the terrain and the dense scrub. These rocky battlements are not high by mountain standards, but our line of march being west to east and all the creeks flowing north to south meant that we were either climbing or descending, never it seemed were we on flat going. The ground was sharp and hard, covered in loose shale which provided little traction. Added to this the bush became thicker. As the afternoon progressed it got hotter, the air seemed filled with all manner of bits and pieces, bark leaves, twigs, flies, spiders and dust. Added to this, every bush, bough, branch, twig and spine wanted either to hold on to me, seeming to enjoy my company, while others poked and prodded or pushed me away. The scrub was always just too high to see over so navigation became difficult. The long afternoon developed into a personal trial with the elements. Despite my object of keeping the Heysen Trail close to the cliff tops we were, bit by bit, being forced inland, the bush and the terrain becoming more demanding the nearer we were to the coast. At some time during the afternoon we must have crossed Arron Creek but I was not conscious of it. Late in the afternoon we reached a track on one of the high ridges somewhere close to where the Trig Campsite is located today. It was abundantly clear that a cliff top route for the Trail was in serious doubt, average walkers would not contemplate such exertions. The cost of constructing the path I felt would be beyond our resources as would the maintenance of such a trail. I also suspected that National Parks would take a jaundiced view of any proposal to clear more native vegetation. We fed on cold rations again, bedded down early determined to have a better day on the morrow, one that would begin with a dawn rise. We rose at the appointed time but whether it was dawn or not I could not say, the area was cloaked in thick sea mist with visibility down to a few feet. We waited nearly 2 hours for that mist to clear, then elected to find the footpath from the end of Tent Rock Road which was then little more than rough track and followed this to the estuary of Deep Creek, and it was there that we had our midday meal. The country from the end of Tent Rock track to the eastern boundary of the park had been ravaged by fire earlier that year and although we did not have to push through the scrub we arrived at Deep Creek in a dreadful state covered in charcoal, black from head to foot. That afternoon was spent in following a most spectacularly scenic ridge that led us back to the coast and that night we camped on Tapanappa Creek where we found an oasis of green with sweet, sweet water amongst the black ruin.

The next day we had to leave the safety of the park and make our way on to Tunkillo Beach. This would have to be done with some care as the beach had recently been the subject of criticism for being described as a private beach and there had been a story doing the rounds about a school teacher who whilst undertaking a similar trip to us was forcibly removed from the beach and that there had been police involvement. I had spent many hours studying the 1:50,000 maps and a new innovation from the Dept. of Lands, a 1:10,000 air photo overlaid with contours and property boundaries. This allowed us to locate the dividing lines between free hold land and crown reserves with pinpoint accuracy and became one of our most useful tools. We descended onto the wave platform and began to make our way towards Tunkillo Beach feeling more like a band of guerilas operating behind enemy lines than walkers. Soon we made our way on to the magnificent 5km of clean white sand untrodden by human feet. The going was hard, the sand providing poor traction and we soon began to walk at the ocean edge where the going was firm, prepared to put up with wet feet and salt encrusted boots. In this way we made good progress, the steep cliffs giving way to rounded downs which form the natural amphitheatre, the background to Tunkillo Beach. By midday we could see Tunk Head clearly standing guardian over the eastern approach to the beach, our next problem.

It was time to lunch, time for another handful of nuts and berries, dried fruit, cheese, and chocolate accompanied by half an aluminium bottle of Tapanappa 1980. It was now three days since I had tasted tea and I could not recall any instance in history where an Englishman had gone so long.

From where we now stood there was a low spit of rock running directly out to sea for perhaps 10 metres already drying to a deep matt blue and it was certainly below the high water mark. If we brewed a billy there it would be safe and it would be legal. I put the scheme to Ian who readily agreed and a few moments later we were sitting on our heels in the time honoured fashion of bushmen drinking our tea.

Ah, tea! It's twenty years since that cup but I can taste it still, made as it was from a tea bag, powdered milk which as always refused to dissolve and seemed only interested in mimicking ice flows and circumnavigating the cup instead of doing its rightful job. We talked of this and that, content with our lot, I facing out to sea, Ian facing me and looking inland. All seemed well when quite suddenly Ian stopped speaking in mid sentence, his eyes began to roll alarmingly in his head his lips working in soundless formations. I thought he must be in the grip of some catatonic fever bought on by the richness of the tea, or was having an impromptu rehearsal for State gurning championships, but then realized in an instant that he was, for reasons best know to himself, engaging me in his own primitive version of the telegraph, and the message was, look behind you! I rose turning as I did so and there just a few metres away was the legendary O'Riley. The O'Riley, aged, weather worn, tall, lean every bit the stockman from the battered Akubra to the RM boots, and Mr O'Riley was not a happy man. There were no introductions, the newcomer got to the nub of the agenda with commendable speed, "you blokes know you're trespassing." The question was put directly and demanded and instant reply. We were looking straight into each others eyes. "No, we're on Crown Land" my voice sounded a lot calmer then I felt. "Maybe, but if that's so, you had to trespass to get here". O'Riley pressed the point. "No we stayed within the coastal reserve all the way here." Neither of us moved. O'Riley changed tack "There's a fire ban in this district and you are breaking the law." "No the stove's below the high water mark and fire bans don't apply". The O'Riley moved closer and pushed the lid back on his head "Well I thought you blokes knew what you were doing when I saw your equipment". All three of us sank to our haunches and we had a good talk. He'd been up on the downs above the beach pulling Scotch Thistles before they seeded when he had spotted us on the sand below and had not thought anything of coming down to check us out. As we were getting on so well I put the rumour about the teacher and the punch up to him, a risky thing, but O'Riley, I never did know his first name, told us his version of the tale and it was a very different one to the city account.

He left us soon after that and the last I ever saw of him was as he strode up the slopes behind the beach. He was nearly 80 at the time.

We climbed over and around Tunk Head with the sea washing the base of the cliffs 100 feet below, determined to stay within the coastal reserve and that night camped on the soft dry sand of Callawonga Beach but once again no drinkable water. The next morning started as usual with a steep climb, this time over to Ballaprudda Beach, another delightful secluded cove. One last heroic climb and we were on relative flat going for the rest of the trip, at first on a clifttop plateau then down a fine spur to the estuary of Coolawang Creek which we waded due to the high state of the tide. We made excellent progress that day, the best of the walk. Passing over first Parsons and then Waitpinga Beach to camp that night on Newlands Head having spent the whole day walking through some of the finest country anywhere. The next day was to be our last, through the coastal scrub of Santa Cruz and over the most spectacular cliffscape we had ever witnessed, then downhill all the way to Kings Head and into Victor to slake our thirsts. We had found no useable water since Tappanapa, neither Coolawang nor Waitpinga Creeks able to supply our needs. Later upon reflection I concluded that the effort had been well worthwhile, an extension of the Trail was certainly feasible and what a trail it would be. It would of course have to swing inland on occasions. I looked forward to getting back on the Peninsula and getting the work started in the next few weeks. As it was, things once more changed and it was almost 4 years before I was back on this finest of coasts.

When I was a boy I read a book called Madagascar Jack which told of the adventures of an apprentice seaman and the afore-mentioned Jack. These two heroes shipped aboard a brigantine out of Nantucket bound for the whaling grounds of the south seas. I was almost a total failure at school, the only thing that they gave me during the whole ten years that I was deposited with them was a love of reading and a retentive memory. I sailed the seven seas with Jack and by the age of 10 years I knew all there was to know of such things as, cutting out spades, try pots, horse bits and blanket pieces and men such as Caleb Kempton, Elihu Coffin and Amos Haskins.

I had never seen a whale and this time I was determined to be on the Peninsula during the whale watching season. This was not difficult to organize and that September, almost four years since our epic walk, saw us, Martin Foster, Bob Bowden and self ensconced in the Yankalilla pub. As you may have already seen I had done a good deal of work already towards the development of the Heysen Trail on the Fleurieu and although it would be a physically demanding job establishing the route, negotiating a right of way did not pose any major problems.

At the same time as Colonel Light was surveying the State in 1836 as well as setting out the road reserves he also instructed his surveyors to reserve a portion of land to be not less than 100 feet from the High Water Mark. This together with two National Parks, Deep Creek and Newlands Head Conservation Parks a slab of Coastal Protection Board land, the beaches at Tunkalilla, Parsons and Waitpinga the rocky foreshore between Cape Jervis and Fishery Beach gave us some formidable bargaining tools.

I had also been a speaker at one of the Fleurieu Agriculture Bureau's meetings. Despite giving me one of my worst experiences as a speaker, I was well received and offered considerable help. What happened was this: I was asked to be one of the guests at the Bureau to introduce the concept of public walking trails in the countryside. There were to be three speakers that afternoon, myself to be the last at 3 o'clock. The other two speakers went on a bit, the first from a bank telling the cockies how difficult it was going to be to borrow money in the future and how interest rates were going to go through the roof. The second speaker was an expert on plant disease and amused us all with stories of hideous plagues that were about to descend on the world accompanied by full colour slides of the effects with frequent assurances that there was no cure. Well by the time these two had finished not only was the meeting well behind time but also most of the members were contemplating mass suicide by casting themselves off Tunk head at low tide! The chairman rose and introduced me and my subject, then one by one the farmers stood and walked out of the hall until only half of the original number remained which did not inspire confidence in me. I was a bit put out by this, even offended. Well, I thought, I am not that bad a speaker. My chagrin must have shown for the Chairman who was sitting next to me whispered a hurried explanation. It seemed that the landowners who had left were dairymen and as milking time came around it was a local convention that they would leave as time and distance dictated. When this misunderstanding was explained to the meeting we all had a good laugh over it, something that they were ready for and I made some solid allies.

The District Council gave its support to the Trail and so I had only to convince the remaining landowners. The first of these was Joe Emanuel. Amongst well known businessmen in South Australia one is Joe Emanuel. the oft told story is of a young Italian immigrant who arrived in Adelaide, started as a market gardener and rose to be one of the State's leading property developers. Joe had a portion of land to the east of the Coast Protection Boards land upon which he erected a holiday home. This home was of a most inappropriate design being shaped like a Martian space ship, not that it seemed to worry anybody. In my humble opinion the house had been built partly on the coastal reserve. The coast in this area was quite low, being little more than 30 metres above the sea but it was indented with small bays and inlets and cut here and there by small creeks, all of which made the unsurveyed coastal reserve both difficult and expensive to identify. I sought and got an interview with the man himself after several weeks of trying. The meeting was to take place at Joe Emanuel's city office high above Rundle Street. I entered the small ultra smart reception room and introduced myself to tall willowy blonde young woman who treated me with an intriguing mix of cool politeness and utter contempt. I was informed with a smile that Mr Angelakis would be with me in a moment. I protested I had come to see Mr Emanuel and not Mr Angelakis. Was there some mistake? I was directed to a seat. A tall well made man of some 30 years entered left and approached me. He smiled a glossy white smile from beneath carefully coiffured jet black hair and offered me a well groomed hand. Joe was busy and he, Mr Angelakis would take me into him as soon as he was free. Mr Angelakis was an amiable chap and we got on well for the few minutes that we waited, then without seeming to have received any advice, Mr Angelakis stood and said that Joe would see us now. I was shown into a large room that overlooked the street and presented to the man himself, who rose from behind his desk and the three of us sat a round a coffee table. I was invited to state my case which I did, horribly conscious that I was doing so for the 32nd time that month and that I was beginning to sound like an action man toy just after you have pulled its string.

I finished off by dropping a hint that Joe's house might be built on public land. He responded in a pleasant enough way telling me that he enjoyed walking and in particular taking his grandchildren for walks and would certainly use the Trail if it were made. He had just one reservation, that the path should be kept at a distance from the house wherever possible and to this I agreed. The maps were spread out on the table and I got the usual blank looks. "Now" said Joe "where do you want to put your Trail?" "You're the landowner" I pointed out "you can tell me where to go, as long as its not to the devil". I've made better jokes in my time, much better, but I've rarely got a better laugh out of one. Joe thought this very funny and the three of us parted on the best of terms.

The way through the Deep Creek Conservation Park took a good deal of planning but the principle of a trail traversing the park had been established long before. As I had found on my 1980 investigation it was just about impossible to keep the path on the cliff tops due to the number of creeks incising the coast and the dense bush that covered most of it. There had been some changes in the park since 1980 and we were very glad to find our old friend Volca Shultz was now the Ranger in charge of the Fleurieu Parks. The fires that had swept through the Park in the early 80's were of no help to us, the scrub had grown back more vigorously than ever. The traditional way for walkers and fishermen to get from Tent Hill to the estuary of Deep Creek had been closed. That had been a sound move on the part of Volca and the Parks Authority, for It was an ill conceived trail made by the army in the years before when the land had still been unalotted Crown Land and there was little management. The camp site on the banks of the Creek had been badly used in the past, but none of this made our job any easier. With the help of Volca we slowly progressed from east to west using existing fire trails, foot path and animal pads and only making new paths where necessary. We were working on the Deep Creek section for several weeks staying at the Yankalilla pub which in those days was not very comfortable for residents. The Fleurieu does not always follow the State weather pattern, tending to have a will of its own. We had good weather for most of our time there but we did run into a spell of cold wet weather that came in from the south and soon had the bush dripping and the creeks running high and we spent two miserable days route finding.

During the afternoon on the second of these days Martin and I were trying to find the best way of taking the way westward from the ridge that runs up to Tapanappa Rocks, to join up with an existing trail that comes down the western side of Deep Creek to a waterfall.

Bob Bowden had been working elsewhere in the district and we had arranged for him to be at the top of the waterfall path at 5 p.m. with the 4-wheel drive. The day went badly from the start, a puncture and a lost key cost us a lot of time. It was nearly 4 o'clock before we heard the muffled grumbling of the falls and looked down the 250 metres through the sodden vegetation and rapidly gathering mist to the Creek below. There was no more time for way finding. If we were to get back to the pub that night we had to get down to the Creek, cross it, and find the path up the 250 metres to our vehicle. We found the Creek so swollen that we had to wade armpit deep across it gripping frantically to any thing that would give even the illusion of security. Somehow we crossed the stream but the Creek was so swollen that there was no bank to follow, the side of the creek climbing straight up out of the water almost vertically. We did the only thing left to do and climbed directly to the ridge top over the boulder strewn escarpment. Thick scrub barred the way, most of it being Kangaroo Thorn. Bob as usual was in the right place at the appointed time, head lights on and sounding the horn at regular intervals. Martin and I staggered gratefully into the vehicle. Half an hour later we were back at the Yank pub only to be informed by the innkeeper that he had forgotten to put the water heater on and that there would be no hot water until 10 30 that night. From then on we made our base at the Hotel Victor preferring to do the extra travelling morning and night.

The Trail made rapid progress from the eastern end of the Park from Tapanappa Creek along Tunkallia Beach to Tunk Head where I had met Mr O'Reilly all those years before. Now we ran into a solid obstacle. A significant portion of the land beyond Tunk Head was owned by a large pastoral company with holdings in other States. I contacted the company's office in Adelaide and after some difficulty, spoke with the Managing Director who was very cool to the proposal, and the call finished without result. Some days later the Department received a long letter from the company telling us of their virtues and the role they played in the economy of the State and the many reasons why a Trail could not be developed on Crown Land that adjoined their holding. The letter went on to say that if further negotiations were to take place then, because of their importance, the talks should take place between the company's managing director and the Minister of Recreation and Sport. It was out of the question for a Minister of the Crown to be placed in such a position and I felt very strongly that as I had been the negotiator since the Trail's beginning that the senior management should get solidly behind me and insist that all negotiations be through me. I put this argument to them as forcibly as I could, but there were other forces at work and it was decided to send two of the most senior men to treat with the company. That they had no experience of negotiating rights of way, no knowledge of the relevant Acts and no background in outdoor recreation and no history of success in the recreation trails area made no difference. They polished their big brass hats and went off to certain defeat and so it proved. The Trail would not follow the cliff tops and there was no avenue for any further discussion about the subject. The project was handed back to me to find a way round, which of course we did, but access to 7km of spectacular coastal cliffscapes and two beautiful secluded beaches had been denied to people who had every right to it.

We met the Lush brothers from Inman Valley and Mrs Barbara Parsons and her family. With their support the Trail went sweeping down Coolawang Creek over Parson's Head along Waitpinga Beach to Newland Head Conservation Park. The Heysen Trail stopped here, there being an embarrassing gap between Newland head and Newland Hill with an unpleasant 10km road bash between the two for some time. This was later resolved in talks with the owners of 'Santa Cruz' and the developer of 'Warradale Park'. The Trail following an age old footpath over maritime crags of outstanding beauty and then turning north toward its ultimate goal, the Flinders Ranges. As for the whales, well one morning I was working in a gully when a call from above brought me scrambling to the headland. "Whale" said Bob Bowden pointing towards the Southern Ocean, and there a kilometre offshore was the silhouette of a whale, a bit disappointing really, I had expected more activity, but then we got some action. The whale hauled up its anchor started its outboard and set a course for Kingscote. No I've never seen a whale.

Shortly after the completion of this section Bob Bowden returned to the Highways Dept. and as Chris Knight had left to pursue her career in the world of horticulture we were back to just two. Things were again tight in the Public Service and we were allowed only one replacement. Andrew Moylan was appointed and from then until the completion of the Trail the team would remain the same. The Heysen Trail was by this time a very long Trail. The project was proceeding well, but the problems were growing. Each part of the Trail we developed needed to be maintained, and there were ever increasing demands for information on all aspects of outdoor recreation.

Communtiy Support

T he support received from the community was overwhelming and could not be ignored, and it was no flash in the pan. It seemed to come from all directions. One morning very early I found myself watching television with my young son. The host went through the usual mindless ritual of children's TV (God you have to admire their nerve) when up came a segment on the Trail. Despite the knockers and the short life of the Trail it was rapidly becoming part of the State's culture. However up until this time the community had had little say in the project and I began to feel that if we wanted to keep up the sort of support we were getting it was time to get walkers at least involved in the planning of the Heysen Trail's future development.

We spent some of our meagre budget on a series of Lands Dept. 1:50,000 topography maps covering the Mt Lofty and Flinders Ranges from Cape Jervis to Parachilna Gorge. We then persuaded Mike Nunan from the Sports unit to lend us an office come shop near the show grounds for a week end. Here we installed the maps in geographic order up one wall right across the ceiling and down another wall. We invited walkers, walking clubs, scouts and just about anyone we thought might be involved. We got a very good turnout with walkers coming and going on both days with plenty of good advice on where the route should and should not go. Over the next few weeks we analysed and distilled the information, until we were able to put a single line on the maps. This line represented the most desirable route for the path, taking in all the best features of the ranges, summits, cliffscapes, valleys views and forests regardless of who owned the land. That was to be our particular problem.

It was now February 1979 and very hot and dry, time to do some research inside. We set out to identify in general terms who owned what and were they likely to be friend or foe. Working through the Lands Department from whom we got the utmost help, we attempted to sort out the land tenure, not that we expected to iden- tify every landholder but to try and see where our friends and enemies were.

I wanted to understand just what we were up against, so we set out to get down onto the maps what was Freehold, Pastoral lease, Perpetual leases, Reservoir reserves, National Parks, Water reserves, Woods and Forest land, Railway reserves, Commonwealth land, School land, District Council reserves, Recreation reserves, and of course unmade Road reserves.

Richard Massey and I spent the hot February days poring over our

51

maps and dashing between the Lands Department and other Government offices, putting the details of land ownership on our master plans piece by piece. At the end of the month we were able to draw a second line on our master map which we called the most feasible route, as opposed to the most desirable. It was very satisfying to see how close the two lines were. But it seemed an awfully long way from Cape Jervis to Parachilna Gorge.

Volunteers had been an essential part of the development of South Australia's trails ever since they had begun. The Adelaide Bush Walkers had marked and made trails in the Flinders Ranges, Mambray Creek and Morialta National Parks. Many of their members had worked on the NFC Trails. The YHA too had done some good work for the NFC as had the Australian Army. The Duke of Edinburgh's Award scheme candidates had also been involved.

As the Heysen Trail began to take shape and rapidly came to the community's notice, Youth Clubs, Church Organisations, Army and Air Force Cadets, most Bushwalking Clubs and many individual walkers wanted to play a part in its development.

It would not have been possible to carry out either the trail development of the NFC or the Heysen Trail without the help of unpaid volunteers. The use of volunteers is however not as straightforward as it would seem at first glance, particularly when you attempt to combine a paid work force with volunteers. Understandably full time staff are often not happy about the situation, they see work that they should be paid to do, being done for nothing and during times of unemployment this is often a cause of tension between the two groups.

There is also the question of discipline, not that I ever had a rigorous military type of regimen in place, but things do have to be done to a plan and things like occupational health and safety regulations must be adhered to and things like confidentiality and a general code of practice and good behaviour. All this needs to be observed, particularly when working with the public.

The Heysen Trail was of a considerable distance by 1985. Maintaining it and continuing to make progress was not possible with volunteers organised on an ad hoc basis.

This was taking more time than it saved. The Heysen Trail was now 600km in length and it all had to be maintained, as well as liaising with land managers.

The amount of paper work was steadily growing. Access agreements and Third Party indemnity agreements had to be dealt with, recorded, answered and filed and by now the Trail was generating its own administrative headaches – Ministerial inquiries.

These were a real pain in the lower regions not that they were so complex in themselves but because of the opportunity that it gave to minor Public Servants who had no real job to make a name for themselves.

They were constantly returning them to the authors for the most simple minded reasons, all the while being very pompous and self righteous about it.

On top of all this we were becoming publicly accepted as the experts on all things outdoor, and were constantly being asked for advice over the phone or by letter about where to go walking with or without a dog, camping, camping equipment, maps and books.

We produced a whole series of give away maps detailing short walks known as 'Jubilee Walks' and a series of advisory booklets under the banner of 'A guide to...', but by 1986 the Trail's development was beginning to slow. Areas of trail that were completed did not have maps and trails were being maintained before they were officially opened. By 1986 the situation was becoming serious and something had to be done.

The Director of Recreation at the time was Graham Thomson, probably the best Director the Department ever had, for Graham had wide experience of Recreation and Sports practice and administration, the only Director who had all three in the 25 years that I was in the Department.

He was also enthusiastic about outdoor recreation and the development of trails.

I discussed the volunteer problem with him and it was agreed that a community support group should be set up. I was voted an additional $3000 to get the project under way.

1986 was of course the State's 150 year Jubilee and we were all keen to play a part and to see that outdoor recreation was seen to be playing a role at the forefront of the celebrations.

The outdoor recreation unit produced a series of brochures detailing 30 short walks in various locations around the State, and I was also serving on two of the Education Dept. Jubilee subcommittees and so it was not until August that I got around to calling a public meeting. The meeting was held in the Dom Polski Centre one Sunday afternoon and attracted over one hundred walkers. We had an array of well known public figures who spoke in glowing terms of the good effects on physical and mental health of the simple pleasure of walking and the need for public access to the countryside.

Warren Bonython, Derek Whitelock, and Kim Mayes the Minister of Recreation at the time, all addressed the gathering. The Bishop of Willochra Brian Rosiea sent a letter of support. The meeting finished by establishing a 'Friends of the Heysen and other Walking Trails Society', with Jim Crinion as its first President. They had the unenviable task of getting the Society organised and taking it from a good idea to a viable and effective organisation which Jim very quickly did.

Jim was followed as President by Neville Southgate, Colin Edwards and Arthur Smith up until the Trail was complete. Graham Thomson made the remainder of the establishment funding left over from organizing the meetings available to the 'Friends' to get themselves started.

Thelma Andersen was appointed as the 'Friends' first executive officer and was to prove to be a tower of strength particularly when securing rights of way for walkers, taking all on comers without flinching. Thelma is not a tall person by world standards and her stature is not of the imposing Aunt Agatha type but I have seen her take on landowners and whole council meetings without flinching and usually winning the day.

The Trails Unit had by now developed enough skills to be able to estimate that the Heysen Trail would take until 1996 if we received no more help, The Trail was completed in 1992 four years ahead of schedule, and that should be the Friends of the Heysen Trail's memorial.

I have some very fond memories of the things we did together and of the great characters I met. Like the building of the Dutch sand ladder over the dunes behind Waitpinga Beach.

The sand ladder was needed to protect the dunes between the beach and the road to Newlands Head Conservation Park from damage by the large numbers of walkers who were expected to use that part of the Trail. The distance was about 500 metres.

The ladder was constructed by laying 4 inch x 4 foot x 1 inch thick permapine planks side by side. As these were being laid, two lines of heavy duty chain were placed over the top of the planks. They were then bolted on to the planks through pre-drilled holes. As this process was going on the ladder was rolled over chain side down.

The planks were all cut and drilled at a workshop we had established at Parks picnic ground, the tools being powered by generators we set up in the Barbecue shelter. We also set up a kitchen there and everyone was kept supplied with hot food and drink.

The job was completed in two days, the cost saving to the Department must have been huge.

One other great feat of Trail construction was the building of a raised walkway the length of Brady's Gully, just north of the old Jupiter gold field. The gully is about 1.5km long and runs slightly downhill. After our success at Waitpinga we turned our thoughts towards the infamous gully and we decided to have a go at building a raised walkway. This became known as an Irish Bog Ladder organised in the same way that had been so successful on Waitpinga Beach, although it was much more complex and a bigger undertaking.

The bog ladder was constructed over a number of weekends and is still in service to this day. It is a joy to use for it lifts the walker up above the surrounding bush and gives another perspective on the Heysen Trail.

There were many other large undertakings by the 'Friends' that are worth a mention but it was the mass of much smaller tasks carried out that got the Trail completed, and up until recent times kept it in top condition.

The 'Friends' also produced some great characters, like Colin Malcolm who was the first Volunteer coordinator of the society. With a small band of 'Friends' a 4-WD and a trailer he formed a trail development flying squad and seemed to be able to complete a huge amount of work in a very short time. Scotsman, Fred Brooks, who became known to us as 'Cossack' because of his love of working on steps, worked tirelessly on his section of the Trail with great enthusiasm, which turned out to be quite infectious.

volunteers hard at work

The story is oft told of the two Irish ladies who hearing of the fame of South Australia's walking trails took their three weeks annual holidays and forsook the Emerald Isles and came down under to sample the finest walking country in the world. Having arrived safely in Adelaide these ladies acquired maps and the other necessities of the walkers trade, and two days after starting out found themselves pushing steeply up a splendid bush covered ridge that rises up out of the valley of the south Para River towards Mt Crawford Fire Tower, a site they were never destined to see. Before these two international walkers could reach the turn off to the tower they had to pass wee

Freddie Brooks and his team working on the path, and of course they stopped to speak, a serious error as it turn out. I passed that way a week later and the two ladies were still on the same trail working away with a will.

Another of the characters was Doug Lean who I first met on the Brady's Creek job.

Doug was a retired carpenter and joiner, a craftsman in other words. He seemed to be everywhere advising and checking the progress of the work. Doug never seemed to go anywhere without a spirit level in hand. Nobody appreciated Doug's fervour for the perpendicular at first, but slowly he showed himself to be one of the most productive section leaders in the 'Friends'.

Alan Colgrave was also the 'Friends' volunteer coordinator , producing vast amounts of work in a quiet unassuming way. Norm Taylor ran the workshop, always doing a top job. Under Norm's supervision trail furniture rolled out of the workshop in great quantities, always on time, where and when it was wanted. Great characters like Bob Percer, Jim Verall, and Tom Thomson emerged to throw their lifetime's skill and enthusiasm into the Trail.

Not all of the characters were good guys of course. There was one who for some reason to which I was never privy, had it in for me, but then being a Public Servant this does happen particularly when you are continually exposed to the community gaze as I was. We began to find waymarkers and information signs appearing on the Trail in the Mt Lofty Ranges close to Adelaide that had obviously not originated from our workshop or complied with our design standards. We put the word out that this had to stop, and so it did but the person responsible clearly continued to think his trail designs were better than ours. This came to light when we were preparing to reconstruct a crossing over Jupiter Creek just south of the old gold field.

We asked for ideas from the 'Friends'. Our phantom sign maker sent in his plan but after costing was done it proved to be impractical. The work was done following a design originating from the Department of Recreation, and the work was duly carried out.

Our friend wrote to the Minister complaining that his method had been ignored, causing great cost to the public purse. A reply was sent explaining the reasons for our choice. This did not however satisfy our man who made a sign explaining his grievance and naming me as the culprit and this was put up at one end of the crossing for all who passed to see. He was not done yet however. At the opening of the walking season at Bridgewater Oval he approached me, the first time we had met, and offered me a plastic bag and insisted that I accept it. Well, I thought a peace offering, a noble gesture indeed and took the bag, opened it to find it contained an assortment of litter, food scraps and cigarette ends. It was, he told me, the litter that he had collected from the Jupiter Creek Crossing after my people had finished the work there and what action was I going to take. I was very annoyed at this, as everyone we had working on the Trails was well aware of their responsibility to the environment. Shortly after this, the gentleman was advised to leave the 'Friends' and he did so.

Black Bob might be gone but he had left us a valuable legacy.

The water tank being built at Spring Creek

Bob was a man fond of his glass and after one wet and difficult day working in the Jupiter Creek Gold Field, Bob repaired to his favourite watering hole, the Hotel Australia in North Adelaide and there fell into conversation with a dark stranger. The conversation, as it does in such situations passed over the weather, the cost of a pint and to their respective means of making their daily bread.

When Black Bob mentioned the Heysen Trail. His imbibing partner started up at this, exclaiming that he was a long time supporter of the Trail but believed the project to have been abandoned in the early 70's. The speaker was none other than Dr. Derek Whitelock, then Reader in Social History at the University of Adelaide.

This chance meeting was to have far reaching consequences right throughout the development of the Trail and beyond. Telephone numbers were exchanged, and shortly after I had my first meeting with Derek. Derek hails from that part of the north east of England which produced the likes of George Stevens and James Boland. A man of sensible height and size with a broad open face that would look well on a yeoman farmer of old. To add to this Derek invariably wears tweed hats, hacking jackets, brogue shoes, always carries a stout stick and is accompanied wherever he goes by a large black pipe. Derek has many interests and is often vocal about them addressing the listener in a rich dark brown voice, the legacy of his Northern birthplace and of his pursuit of knowledge at both Oxford and Cambridge.

This meeting started a whole chain of events that spread the word on the Heysen Trail far and wide and kept the project in the eyes of Ministers and politicians. There were Heysen Trail University adult education schools, two radio series, Heysen Trail picnics, numerous articles, letters to newspapers and introduction to Derek's then wife Carole who was on the verge of radio fame.

Bill Reschke was one of the Heysen Trails most formidable supporters. I had known Bill for some years, when we were members of the Tilbruky Trail Committee, a proposal to construct a footpath from Kingston Park to Cape Jervis following the dreaming trail of the Kaurna people's legendary hero, Tjilbruki. When it became obvious that the Trail was not going very far, the NFC interest could not be sustained, but Bill doggedly carried on doing splendid work with John Downey, getting a monument constructed at Kingston Park and identifying the many weeping sites along the way.

Bill was from one of the old River Murray families at Mannum and had a deep and abiding love of the land. When we met he was already famous for his River Murray Pilot, and still keeps a cruiser up at Mannum.

Bill had served in the RAAF working on airstrips in the far north of Queensland. These had given him a great love of the outdoors and a deep respect for Aboriginal people. When it became known that the Heysen Trail was to be constructed, Bill was there reporting on the first stage in the Cleland Conservation Park in 1974.

When the Trail proper got started Bill was once more on the ground. Bill was a journalist of the old school, he'd learned his trade at the London office of Reuters just after World War II. The story of his time as the press liaison officer with the British civil service's White Fish Authority. is far funnier than the 'Yes Minister' series.

Reschke is a man of slight stature, boney, with a thin inquisitive face, a man who seemed to have little concern for his own physical comfort.

I remember hearing of one occasion when he flew as navigator in the open cockpit of a Tiger Moth half way across the continent in the middle of winter just to get a story. Bill never shied away from the hard stuff, always wrote his columns on first hand experience. When he wrote the stories on the Trail he'd been there, whether on the south coast over Mt Remarkable, through the Flinders or even at a meeting of graziers in the Blinman pub. He always wrote big, usually centre page with plenty of bold photographs, taken by him or Brian Webber. Bill wrote the whole story warts and all. His contribution to the successful outcome of the Trail cannot be calculated. We were all very pleased to see Bill, looking fit and well at the opening of the Trail in 1992.

Kym Tilbrook was a supporter of the Heysen Trail from its beginning. Kym hails from the country town of Clare in the State's mid north. He has a deep love and respect for the Australian landscape, loves to walk its ranges, enjoys writing of his experience and passing on his enthusiasm to others. When I first met Kym he was The Advertiser's political roundsman and a founding member of the Adelaide Gentleman's Walking Club.

During the 1980s Kym became the editor of The Advertiser's highly successful 'Getting Out' monthly feature magazine. The progress on the Heysen Trail was regularly reported on by Kym. This kept the project in the public eye and in the eye of the Government.

One morning quite early there appeared in the Department of Rec. and Sport a grey clad figure who was quite unknown to any of us. This tall lean apparition announced himself as one Douglas Paice, representing the Government Printer. He was there to see to our printing wants. This I must tell you did not impress any of us. At this time in the history of the Public Service the Government Printer ran an efficient and competitive organisation, staffed by some of the country's finest printing craftsmen. Each Department had a representative from the printer who liaised with various department managers to get the best results.

I had however never got on well with the previous reps for a variety of reasons, most of which were my fault. The printer's trade is a complex one and if you can master it after surviving a seven year apprenticeship you have the right to feel somewhat superior to lesser mortals, particularly if those mortals spend their time clomping about the bush in large boots and apparently producing nothing. The previous reps had always talked in a language that I could barely comprehend. They spoke of Heildelbergs and colour separations, widows and orphans, trannies, choirs, reams and galley proofs.

They had had the very annoying habit of assuming that because I understood nothing of the printer's art that I therefore had the IQ of a house brick. They then wanted to rewrite and edit my written work, this was simply not their role and it caused deep resentment.

Doug did not get an easy start with us but this did not last for long. Not only did he know the printing trade but he also had the ability to relate to his clients and as a bonus Doug was an enthusiastic bushwalker.

Doug took responsibly for getting the maps and all associated publications designed and printed, keeping the price down and the quality up during most of the development of the Heysen Trail.

Kapunda Meeting

As we progressed north towards Kapunda I was invited to address yet another meeting of landowners. Well, you should read the chapter on public meetings. In truth this was not so bad but the general feeling was that they did not want the Trail in their council area. The message was at least delivered with some dignity and without rancour. After the usual two hours of verbal to-ing and fro-ing I had not been able to win a single concession out of them.

The landowners assured me that there was much better walking country to the east, to the west and all other points of the compass. In fact it transpired that the Kapunda area was one of the worst walking districts in the country and was well known for it.

They assured me that they supported the Trail and all deeply regretted that they did not have suitable land on which to locate it. To show their goodwill, they offered that if we located the Heysen Trail outside of their Council District they would not object to its development.

It was by now getting near to closing time, feet were beginning to shuffle, chairs scrape and time pieces were carefully examined with exaggerated taps of fingers on glass, held up to ears and shaken, all done when the Chairman was looking at the appropriate part of the hall. Finally the Chair took the hint and called for one last question, a hush fell over the room all were now eager to leave, then from the back of the hall there was a stirring. Slowly there rose a tall spare framed man, weather worn, lean and of advanced years, all heads turned towards him. He addressed himself directly to me and spoke without regard to the meeting "Mr Lavender my name is Con Huppatz", he introduced himself in the thin wavering voice which carried throughout the hall. He went on "I am the owner of Peters Hill Station. From the top of Peters Hill there are views in every direction I think that people from the city should be able to see those views. I will be very disappointed if the Heysen Trail does not cross my land". The meeting broke up shortly after but few people left. Suddenly I was in demand, the Trail seemed to have lost its bad reputation, dour landowners were ready to talk, Con Huppatz' few words had done more for the Trail than all my efforts during the rest of the night. Mr Huppatz was as good as his word. It was always the case that I would be some weeks in front with my negotiations and It took time before the work crew caught up with me. A few weeks later I was sitting at my desk when a phone call from the reception informed me that I had a visitor. On going to the front desk I was surprised to find that Con Huppatz was my visitor. He told me that he was disappointed that he had not heard from me further since the meeting. During the next few months and years I was to meet Con, his wife, and son James. I visited their home at Riverton and was shown around the property and James told of their families and their European origin, all with great pride.

The Huppatz family continued to support the Trail from then on. Later when we were planning the Trail through the mid north we found that the Trail would pass through another section of land owned by the Huppatz family. They gave their permission without hesitation and later we built huts on both holdings, restoring at one location the original homestead, something that the family took great interest in. They were always ready to get stuck in when there was hard work to be done. It was a great privilege to have known them.

The 9th section of the Trail was now complete. Winding its way out of the Barossa Range across the valley floor through the village of Greenock over Mt Belvedere to briefly visit Kapunda then across country over Peters Hill to just south of Mirrabell, home of the Rodeo. The stuffed head of Spitfire, its most famous son. now adorns the front bar of the pub. It must be the most inept piece of taxidermy in the southern hemisphere.

Mt Lofty to the Barossa Range

With the ending of the Aboriginal and SYETP funding, Richard and I were once more on our own but we now had a 4-wheel drive and a reasonably equipped workshop.

I set about trying to find more staff, and with the help of Brian Taylor the Director of the Division, a man who always gave me his support, I was able to get Martin Foster and Peter Scapinelli on to the staff. Martin stayed with the project right though until the complete trail was opened in 1993. He had the same sort of inventive genius as Richard Massey with a touch of the avant garde thrown in.

Martin was also a fair hand at sign writing. We had a whole series of bizarre animal heads, posters and gadgets appear at the workshop. One that always sticks in my mind is the Martin Foster patent key holder. At this time we were collecting a range of keys and I suggested that Martin might try his hand at knocking up a keyboard to store the unused keys. I was thinking along the lines of a few cup hooks screwed into a piece of wood. When I returned to the workshop a few days later I was presented with a carefully made model of a piano keyboard complete with six cup hooks.

Peter Scapinelli started a few days later than Martin. Peter was a big chap, an ex footballer, strong as a horse and a willing one at that, with some considerable woodworking skills.

His lasting monument is the deep hole toilet he designed and built at the Mylor Baptist light weight camp site near the village of Mylor.

The popularity of the Trail continued to grow and we were soon looking at the next section which I decided would be an extension from Mt Lofty to Tweed's Gully at the southern end of the Barossa Valley.

This part of Mt Lofty is probably the most rugged, it is also close to Adelaide. One of the great things about living in Adelaide is the way that the suburbs end and the bush starts at the bottom of the Mt Lofty Ranges.

I had worked extensively throughout the district with a bloke called Ted Lovegrove during the early 1970's on a network of trails for the NFC, a development which had proved very popular, but the footpaths were being neglected and were slowly mouldering away.

I decided to use some of the routes from the network for the extension of the Heysen Trail. This gave me two immediate advantages, I knew the trails, and had a few years to contemplate the improvements that could be made and I had already got to know the landowners. With the help of the Woods and Forest Dept. and the National Parks and Wildlife Service we made some significant changes to the existing trails particularly over Thomas Hill and through the Montacute Conservation Park.

We soon had a rugged and spectacular route for the Trail to the Barossa Valley. We found it impossible in the short term to avoid some sections of bitumen particularly around Norton Summit and at Cudlee Creek. The question therefore was, did we open the next part of the Trail or wait until it was all off road? I decided against this, there was only about 4km of made road out of the 80km of trail on this section. Public support was running high but we still had enemies; there were still people who would have preferred to see even our modest funding put into other areas. We went ahead, marked the Trail, erected the Trail furniture, and wrote, designed and published our second brochure.

One of the best parts of working on the trails was the varied characters that always cropped up in each district we worked in and this one was no exception. A few kilometres north of Kersbrook the Trail would have to leave the Simmonds Hill forest and cross the steep grazing property of Milton Checker. Milton had allowed me to locate one the old NFC trails over his land and he did so once again. The Checker family must have been one of the first to settle in the district. Milton, a tall lean craggy man was the Mayor of the Gumeracha District Council for many, many years and always a great community supporter.

To the north of Milton's place was Bill Levitt's land. Bill was a fanatical lawn bowler to such a degree that he had his own bowling green at the side of the farm house including lights.

I also renewed my acquaintance with Ian Ross, the Chairman of the Barossa District Council. I first met him during the development of the NFC Trails. He was, like a lot of the cockies I met, deeply tanned, lean and hard looking. In fact he was very open handed with the use of his property. After the Heysen Trail was developed across his land we restored the original farmhouse as a walkers hut. Some years later I upset Ian over a subdivision matter which is something that I still regret.

We organized the second grand opening of the Heysen Trail and the new Minister John Bannon agreed to do the honours. It was one of the worst mid-winter's days for years when we gathered at the Cleland Conservation Park. The crowd included Government officials, walkers, Parks staff, and a good turnout by the media including all three TV news programmes.

I introduced myself, welcomed the guests and introduced the Minister and there we stood, a semi circle of black and brown Japara, a thick mountain mist providing the background.

It was dense, almost solid, except where it touched bush and body and turned instantly to ice cold rivulets, there to find its way to the ground via neck and wrist.

The Minister, good humored almost boyish, spoke of the Government's support for the Trail, their belief in outdoor recreation, then opened the new section of trail by unveiling a brass plaque. Relief was at hand, the Minister invited everyone to join him for tea in the visitors centre and off they trooped.

The Trail on 'Princess Royal' south of Burra

I remained behind to recover the flag but before I could make my way into the warm and dry I was approached by the camera operator from the ABC who confided in me that she had failed to load the camera with film, and consequently she and the ABC crew had nothing to show for their morning's work and would not be popular back at Collinswood. It was now 3pm I had been on duty since 8am and I was damp and cold. I was missing English soccer on the box, what could I do? Well how about asking the Minister to come back, you introduce him and he gives his address again. It was with some misgivings that I approached John Bannon, later to be Premier, took him aside and explained the problem and its proposed solution.

The Minister did not hesitate and a few minutes later we were back in the mist and performed the whole thing again.

That night all three television news programmes covered the Heysen Trail.

Peters Hill to Newikie Creek

We were now beginning to get into country that had never been popular with walkers, in fact I had never spoken to any walker who had used the area. We spent a week exploring the district mostly around the Tothill Range which lies in country to the east of the Riverton Burra road and goes due north to Burra. It was hardly known to anyone outside of the district, yet walking there in the early spring of that year was a delight. The Tothill Range never reaches more than 700 metres in height yet it is rugged, twisted and incised. Viewed from the east its scrub covered peaks stand out against the sky line, a black saw toothed range.

Having decided that the area was worthwhile I opened talks with the District Clerk of the Eudunda Council, got a good reception there and was passed on to the Chairman of the Council, a substantial landowner in the area whose family also held parts of the Tothill Range. During our investigations of the area we had found that there were a series of unmade road reserves and 4-wheel drive tracks at the base of both the eastern and western flanks of the Range. We also discovered that several of the properties had been taken up by absentee landlords who lived in Adelaide. These proved to be uncommunicative rather than uncooperative and obviously without any understanding of the road reserve situation. The locals on the other hand were more concerned with the protection of the unique vegetation on the summit ridge of the range than with anything else. I was hoping to do some sort of land swap between the reserves at the base of the Range and the ridge top. But a single walk along the ridge convinced me that this would be the wrong thing. The vegetation was in good condition but putting a public footpath in conflict with the conservation of native plants and animals was not a battle we could ever put our hearts into, and not one for which we would get community support. However as much as I agreed with conservation sentiments I still wanted the Trail to take advantage of the wonderful views there were to be had on either side of the range. A compromise was soon worked out.

The Trail would mainly occupy the reserves at the base of the range but so as to take advantage of the views over the surrounding country the Trail would climb over the Range at four gaps or passes and this has worked well ever since.

From Tothill Gap the Trail climbed steadily up over a shallow watershed into another property owned by the Huppatz Family and down to the Robertstown Road along an interesting section of trail that provides many good sections of easy walking.

Where the Heysen Trail crosses the Burra to Robertstown Road is the area known as Logan's Gap where Logan's Creek flows down to Burra Creek. The road was at one time part of the Adelaide bullock track down which the drays of copper must have passed in the early days of the colony. From here it is just about 20km to Burra, crossing Burra Creek then up on to the main range and over Stein Hill all of it over just two properties The Gap and Princes Royal. I always liked the look of the country around here although I had never met anyone who had walked over it.

I went first to the owners of The Gap Station who received me with a very warm welcome The property owner's son had recently married a local girl and his mother and father had decided to retire and move into town and let the young couple run the station, and so this was a happy time for all of them. The route that I proposed for the Trail was accepted and I was also given keys to the gates and allowed to take the 4-wheel truck on to the property which made life very easy. Now I had to convince the owners of Princes Royal to do the same. Princes Royal is a fair size for that part of the world and I had to drive all the way to Burra just to get to the front gate. Then almost as far south again to get to the home of Alan Slade the property manager, passing as I did the imposing stone station house. I did not feel at all confident about these negotiations. The property seemed very large and prosperous. There was plenty of stock around and everything looked neat, tidy and well cared for, and of course I knew that the owner lived in Adelaide, visiting the stations only at weekends.

My misgivings were unfounded, for Alan Slade was a friendly straight forward bloke, but better than that he was a walker and a leader in the Scout Association. Provided we took all the usual precautions against , fire, third party risk, gates, and located the path away from houses, sheds, mills, tanks, water points and generally keep the Trail to the least productive areas of the property, then we could go ahead and plan the route. Alan offered to talk to Mrs Tennant the owner of the station the following day. I returned to the office, waited a couple of days then phoned the owner, Mrs Tennant. Yes, Alan Slade had spoken to her and yes she was agreeable to the Trail crossing Princes Royal, and I was to liaise directly with Alan. Another long stretch of the way agreed upon, we could now start looking for the route north of Burra.

A week later I received another call from Mrs Tennant, her accountant had advised her not to allow the Heysen Trail to pass through the property and she felt that his advice should be taken. So I was back at Logans Gap no further forward than I had been weeks before, worst still was the fact that all the good work done with 'Gap' families would be useless if the path could not traverse Princes Royal. We began our work over again looking east and then west of the range hoping to find a suitable alternative, a task at which we had only moderate success. It was my habit at this time to talk to Warren Bonython regarding the progress the Trail was making and get his views on the proposed route. I mentioned the disappointing result from Princes Royal and my brief discussion with Mrs Tennant. Warren then told me that his family had known the Tennants during his younger days more than 50 years before. I suggested to Warren that perhaps if a meeting could be arranged between himself and Mrs Tennant he might overcome her objections or at least her accountant's objections. So it was a few days later that Thelma Andersen, Warren, and myself met Mrs Tennant at her palatial residence at Medindie. We spent a pleasant hour together by which time an agreement was reached. The Heysen Trail could pass through the property for a trial period of two years and would then be reviewed. Mrs Tennant made the observation that I looked like a man who might know his way around a bar and when I agreed. I was directed to what I took to be double doors leading to the next room but on opening them found it to be the cocktail cabinet. We sealed the bargain in large gins all round. The following week found us three walking over the steep barren ridges to the summit of Stein Hill. The way was now clear to Burra.

Newikie Creek to Spalding

This was the longest length of trail between habitations; a distance of over 100km over some very rough and remote country that did not seem to me to have received much attention from the walking fraternity, yet the further we delved into it the more fascinating it became. One of the comments made by walkers during our consultation period was that there were no good walking areas in the mid north and that it would be a waste of public money to develop a footpath in that district. This seemed to be based on the belief that there was nothing worthwhile north of the Barossa Range until you get to Crystal Brook, yet we had found some very enjoyable areas in our investigations. It had long been my tactic to stay in the North Mt Lofty Ranges and get as close to Crystal Brook as possible before turning to the west and I was sure that if we did this we could find an interesting way over Mt Bryan through Hallett to Spalding, but for now our objective was to get from Burra to Hallett. The District Councils both supported the Heysen Trail development and the District Clerks and their staff gave us great help with names of landowners and directions of where to find them. We were going to need all the help we could get on this section of Trail, and get it we did but from some unexpected sources.

I never did rise to the exalted level of Director of Recreation and I don't think it even crossed anyone's mind that I could do the job;

odd, when you think of how many Directors the Dept. had, and a very mixed lot they were too. During the time I was working in the Flinders Ranges the current Director came to me and said he intended to come to Blinman the next time we were there and see what we got up to. Most office bound staff tended to think that we had a great life walking all day and carousing the night away at the public's expense and getting paid to do so. When the next trip came around I went and saw the top man and told him when we were leaving and he said that that was fine and he'd come up and have a look at us. So I said, "could you let me know what days you will be there so that I can book your accommodation". "Accommodation" he exclaimed, "you don't think I can afford to spend the whole day with you do you?" Now here was a man born and bred in South Australia with all the qualifications and leadership qualities that I was told that I lacked, who believed that Blinman was just the other side of Smithfield. The only other director we had to take it into his mind to 'have a look at us' was John Miller who did come and join us as we were starting to look at the country south of Newikie Creek. The country in that area is very steep and undulating and provides some particularly good walking although often hard going. We found some unmade reserves running through it, although few had fences intact. It was while we were investigating these reserves that John chose to join us.

The Public Service Board always seemed unhealthily obsessed with time keeping and with the number of hours we put in, whereas the old NFC had trusted its officers to get on with the job and was much more concerned with results than the filling in of time sheets. Some time before I arrived at the Dept. they had introduced a new time management system for officers in my situation, and that was known as 'Time in Lieu'. It was supposed to work like this. You were contracted to work 150 hours per month, nominally $37^1/_2$ hours per week, however if your duty required you to work longer than this you then had to take off the overtime within the next month. The problem was that most officers that I knew either had more work than they could do in $37^1/_2$ hours or were enthusiastic enough, or both, to want to get on with their jobs. In the end this usually meant that the Government got vast amounts of unpaid overtime. The really annoying thing about this was that while all of this unpaid effort was going on we were continually under fire as being bludgers and there were always moves going on to bring in time clocks and make us more accountable. It was John Miller joining us for the week in the Ranges north of Burra who reminded me of a typical working week away from the office. We arrived in the district at about 10am and set out on our investigation and did not meet with our prearranged transport until 5:30pm. It was then 6:30pm by the time we had driven to the pub. John suggested drinks in the bar, a pleasure that I had to forgo as I was addressing a meeting of landowners at Marrabel at 8pm and so had only time to change, fill the Landcruiser with fuel and head south.

My meeting did not finish until 10:30pm and all was dark and quiet by the time I got back to the Pub. The next morning we were on the road by 8:30am and back trying to find a suitable route for the Trail north of Newikie Creek. This did not go well and our progress was very limited. Once more at the end of day I had only time to change , no dinner again, and then off to Crystal Brook to a meeting with local councilors and landowners. I got back to the hotel heralded only by the rich nasal chorus of the replete. The poor results of the day before required an early start the next day. Now this may not seem like the Public Service of popular belief. Why not simply stay on an extra day or come back another time? Maintaining four public servants even at a modest pub is expensive and we had to work within a tight budget. Every expenditure had to be made to get the maximum result. We had a much better day, and it now seemed the sort of route we thought worthwhile. Back at the hotel things were not so good. I went into the bar this time with every intention of claiming the long promised drink off the Director but before I could order the landlady handed me a message; Alex Fisher a landowner to the south with whom I had already finished negotiating had had a change of heart and would I call on him that night? Once again the Director's pint eluded me. I did get dinner for the first time in three days and was soon on my way down little known byways looking for a remote farm that I had only visited once before and then in the day time. Alex had not changed his mind about the Trail but just the route or a part of it to which I had no objection but this meant that his neighbor had to be consulted. A quick phone call might just do it, but no, the neighbor did not want to talk about it over the phone so back on the road further south and further away from an early night. We finally finished that week's work at 4pm on the Friday afternoon and then drove home. I had worked over 60 hours that week and it was not that unusual. Yet, right up until I left the Public Service the senior management was still advocating more stringent time control for officers, with the exception of themselves of course. All this was going on just at a time when industry and commerce were adopting more flexible working hours and encouraging staff to work from home and putting in faxes, e-mail and personal computers.

We found the country north of Burra made good walking, being surprisingly varied, particularly between the stark moorland beauty of the ranges to the west of Monglarta to the much more heavily wooded land around Wiry and Newikie Creeks. To the north of Newikie Creek the hills became very steep and difficult, eventually forcing us to follow Caroona Creek out on to the plain at the foot of the eastern escarpment. I often found that when negotiating a right of way with a landowner that the strangest thing could effect the outcome of the talks and this is what happened here. I had arranged to meet Mr Brian Simmonds at his farmhouse and arrived there in the company of Andrew Moylan at the appointed time. Mr Simmonds had not welcomed my advances on the telephone and was even more hostile in the flesh. The meeting took place in the open air of the farm yard in the midst of an assortment of abandoned vehicles and farm machinery. The talks were getting nowhere, when Andrew, who had been silent up to this point, waited for a pause in the debate then asked "Is that the chassis of an FC Holden?", pointing to a shapeless piece of junk off to one side. "Why yes" said the landowner, "and I've got the rest of it in the shed if you're interested", and so they went off in raptures of delight into the shed. Later Mrs Simmonds bought me out a glass of cold orange juice and we chatted of this and that. After some time the two car buffs emerged from the dark of the shed. Well pleased with the morning's work they shook hands and arranged to meet at Andrew's place the next weekend and prepared to depart, the cocky into the house and Andrew in to the Toyota. "Um what about the Trail" I called after him "Oh" said the cocky "It'll be OK take it along my boundary fence."

This advance brought us out on to the foot of the Range where we intended to go north for about 5km. This was the most northerly point of the Trail in the Mt Lofty Ranges. It was at this juncture that the way was to turn to the west climbing through the range via the spectacular Tourilie Gorge, one of the finest in the State although almost unknown at the time. Before we could pass through Tourilie Gorge I would have to make my peace with Bert Thomas the owner of Hog Back Station. We had got on much faster on that field trip than I had expected and had not even anticipated going on to Hog Back and so had no previous contact with them. However I wanted to keep the momentum going if I could. Later that afternoon I called at the Burra District Council Offices seeking details on Hog Back and left shortly afterwards with directions on how to get there and the telephone number. During the evening I made several calls to Hog Back and more in the morning without success and so decided to go out there unannounced, which was against our usual practice. Hog Back Station is a large grazing run which occupies salt and blue bush country with its western boundary at the foot of the Mt Lofty Ranges some 25km to the east of the town of Hallett. The Station gets its name from an oddly shaped hill that rises out of the plain to the north west of the homestead, and with the fairly free use of the imagination a person unfamiliar with the porcine species might conclude that it looked a bit like a pig.

Hog Back is a remote station and we were directed to drive 40km east of Burra and then pick up a back track and drive on another

The tranquility of Crystal Brook

25km north and there we would find Hog Back. Oddly enough we did. The homestead itself was a typical station building, single story, shallow gabled roof an all round verandah supported by oversized columns. The place was sadly run down in fact it looked as if it was slowly mouldering back in to the earth. Bert Thomas his wife and another woman were taking it easy sitting under the verandah enjoying a noonday beer as we drew up. I made the introductions and hands were shaken, then much to my surprise Bert said "yes I got your letter OK and I am happy for you to go ahead". The simple fact of life was that until the day before I had not heard of Bert Thomas or Hog Back Station and had certainly never written to him, but nothing that I could say would change his mind. So I simply went through the proposal despite his protests, at the end of which he told me that I could do any thing I wanted on that side of the property as he had no intention of ever stocking it in the future. Bert told us that we had come the long way round and described to us a quicker way back to Burra via the property's back tracks. We shook hands and parted. For the next four hours we took the grand tour of Hog Back through a maze of little used station tracks in featureless country amongst head high bush.

The next landowners were of quite different ilk. Tourilie Gorge was the key to this part of the Trail, the only alternative being a 4-wheel drive track to the south. We had found out that there was a road reserve running through the gorge, a legacy from the time many years before when there had been a mine there. The property to both the north and the south of the gorge was owned by the same people. The owners lived in the Mt Lofty Ranges and travelled overseas for much of the time. My approach was first by letter and then a telephone conversation with the lady of the family. Following this I was left in no doubt as to their opposition to the Trail. I pointed out that the land on which I intended to locate the Trail was in fact public land, and was then referred to their solicitor. The solicitor turned out to be a QC, which I felt was a bit of overkill just to get the better of a humble public servant. However, he turned out to be a friendly sort of bloke and we spent a pleasant day walking in the gorge and I was able to show him the situation at first hand, and all seemed to be plain sailing from there on. A few days later I was surprised to receive a letter telling me that unless I desisted from marking the Trail through the gorge court action would be taken against me, the Director of the Department and the Minister of Recreation and Sport. The decision was of course the Minister's. Kym Mayes had no hesitation in ordering me to proceed. The Trail passed through the gorge, up a very steep pinch off the plain and back into the Mt Lofties. This part of the ranges makes great walking but there is little other access than the Heysen Trail. It is probably the most remote part of the Trail, set in stark, uncompromising, brooding country. The views from the top of the scarp looking to the east towards the River Murray are truly magnificent. The locals tell me that although you can't see the river, in the days of the wood burning river boats, you could see the smoke from their chimney stacks on the sky line. From here the way turns west and begins its ascent of Mt Bryan, easily at first, passing the old Mt Bryan East School. It was a long abandoned ruin when we first passed it by, but destined to be restored into a splendid hut. The climb up to the summit of Mt Bryan is a hard one from the east but the effort is well rewarded by some of the most amazing views to be found anywhere. The Trail now takes a long easy swoop into Hallett.

We now faced one of the most difficult route finding problems. How to get the Trail from Hallett to the Spalding Channels. The first 20km did not pose much of a problem, there were several worthwhile reserves, mostly unused, and crossing rolling countryside. A good mixture of grazing and cropping land. However from this point there was no help from road reserves and it seemed that our only option was to follow a very broad fairly dull road at the base of the Brown Range and then follow the Spalding to Burra Road, about 18kms all of which would be on a broad gravel surface through quite mediocre country. This would not be acceptable to walkers. We decided to take a break and do some more research in an attempt to find a more acceptable alternative way for the Trail to pass.

If you have ever driven to the Flinders Ranges for a walking holiday and taken the scenic route through the Clare Valley, Spalding and then via Gladstone you will, just after leaving Spalding, pass over the Bundaleer Channels. If you have not noticed them, don't feel badly for it takes only a moment's lack of concentration to miss one of the Mid North's great wonders. Towards the end of the 19th.

century the demand for water in the mid north for both farming and also mining at Wallaroo and the surrounding district was rapidly on the increase. The Beetaloo reservoir was constructed in 1890 to impound water for these areas but could not meet demand except after a very wet season. The Bundaleer Reservoir was commenced in 1898 to supplement the mid north supply. To assist with the gathering of water for the dam 26kms of channel were constructed to bring water from the creeks to the north and south of the dam. This is an amazing story, in itself one too long to tell here, suffice to say that over 500 men lived and worked on the channels. That the channels drop only 1 yard in 1mile and were made with only the most primitive tools is a remarkable feat.

In more recent times the Bundaleer Reservoir has become less important and the channels are rarely used. The first suggestion that the channels could be used to accommodate the Heysen Trail came from Don Wilsdon the proprietor of Geralka Farm just south of Spalding. Don had been a long serving member of the Long Distance Trails Committee until April 1978 when it held its last meeting. Don argued that the Channels could offer a connection from the Property of Oban to the south of Spalding through to the weir on Never Never Creek, a distance of more than 25km. Should we be able to get the cooperation of the Engineering and Water Supply Department there would also be the possibility of camping sites. We met Graham Hogbin the man who controlled the district for the E&WS and after some hard negotiating the E&WS not only agreed to the use of the Channels for the Heysen Trail but also handed over the ownership of the southern Channels to the Dept. of Recreation and Sport for the further development as a recreation reserve. We were therefore committed to using as much of the channel system as possible. The further north we went with the path the less the likelihood of using the Channels south of Spalding. On the other hand if we went to the south it would mean missing out on the country between Newikie and Caroona Creeks, Tourilie Gorge and the most spectacular ascent of the summit of Mt Bryan. I went looking to the north but was not overjoyed at the prospects and met some stiff opposition, not that that would have deterred us if the rewards had been high enough. In the meantime Andrew pointed out that there was still the possibility of following the old dry stone wall south along the Brown Range which if it could be pulled off would give us a 14km walk over a low but impressive ridge traversing Mundunnie and Mungoowie Hills. The problem was that the country was all freehold with no public land anywhere near so we would be entirely at the tender mercies of the owner. Andrew had met the landowners at some previous time. These included Messrs. Summerville, Mundunie, Norton and Bailey and felt that he might stand a chance. It was worth a go, the owner might be another

FC Holden fanatic. Andrew set out on his mission impossible. He put the scheme to the farmers and got an agreement. The Trail made another huge jump forwards taking it to the weir at Never Never Creek.

The Trail got a good reception north of the weir although at one stage I doubted it. The owner I wanted to see, Mr Ian Radford lived in a shallow valley on a tributary to Never Never Creek. It was up this creek that I found my way early one morning and soon came upon the house which was set low into the hillside blending into the side of the creek more like the home of Bilbo Baggins than a station homestead. As I drew near, the place seemed more imposing, the windows were dark, green mould tinged the flag stones and the abundant vegetation was hanging heavy with moisture from the low verandah. There was a strong sense of decay about the place and my instinct was to slip quietly away and come again in the company of others. Before I could take any action there came a disembodied voice "What can I do for you mate?" and from behind the corner water tank stepped a young chap of about 30 years of age. It is difficult to explain something as complex as the Heysen Trail quickly and be understood, but I managed. "That's a great idea" said the young chap, "Jump in my wagon and I'll show you around the place". We spent the next 2 hours bouncing and bucketing around his country over ridges down gullies and across creeks. It seemed to me to be a very tough land to have to make a living out of, but the young bloke was full of enthusiasm. He gave a running commentary on his management strategy as we went and also found time to give me a short course on something called hybrid vigour.

I was then passed on to the next property owner. The Trail followed Never Never Creek north for 12km all the way to the Bundaleer Forest and we were received with the same enthusiasm by all the landowners along the way. Erwin Shilton was the Forest Ranger at the Bundaleer forest and he guided us through the area to the summit of New Campbell Hill. We could clearly see the South Flinders Ranges over 20km away and the Bluff. On the very edge of vision the great hump of Mt Remarkable could also be discerned.

From the base of the range there was nothing else for it but to plod the 5km of dust and gravel to Georgetown. At least it had the saving grace of arriving at the door of the pub. We found splendid walking country from Georgetown, dropping 200 metres into the beautiful serpentine valley of Rocky River and on to Crystal Brook. Bowmans Park lies across the Brook some 5km north east from the town and it was to there I journeyed to negotiate a right of way for the Trail through the Park. I had previously met with Ted Merton the manager, sometime before during the late afternoon of a perfect spring day. Ted was already familiar with the concept of the Trail, having heard me speak at a meeting of landowners in "The Brook" some time before. We very quickly reached an agreement and began to talk of other things. Ted asked me if I was in a hurry to get away and to my lasting regret I answered, "no" as Ted then invited me to help him with the milking. Well that sort of thing was never in my job specification and I wondered what the bowler hat brigade at the Public Service Board would think of this. Ted led me across the oval to a small green shed which I assumed housed some species of goat which he wanted me to wrestle to the ground while he extracted its milk. On reaching the shed Ted bade me wait outside and went into its interior only to reappear not towing a nanny, but carrying a large calico bag which had an ominous bulbous shape. My worst fears were confirmed when Ted upended the bag and tipped out at our feet a large and rather annoyed Brown Snake. "He's a bit agro mate I only captured him this morning". I was about to flee when Ted advised we not to make any sudden moves. Any sudden moves!! Good God this was my worst nightmare come alive. When I was a small boy I was put to the study of Greek myths. One of the least loveable characters was a lady called Medusa who had in place of hair venomous vipers. The story which I had previously had some doubts about, went on claiming that anyone who looked at her would be turned to stone. Well, I can tell you now from first hand experience that this is no myth, it happened to me, albeit with only temporary effect, but it happened!! I rarely visit Bowman Park any more although people tell me it has come on wonderfully well in the last few years. Somehow I never feel at ease there.

Barossa Range to Peters Hill

In 1986 I started to push the Trail on from the Mt Crawford area towards the Barossa Valley then north through Kapunda and on towards the Tothill Range. On this section I was to receive some of my greatest support and some very severe and unpleasant opposition, which was destined to turn into a running battle that may well be going on to this day. The way north east was quite straight forward, east along a double fenced fire access trail then down a dirt road to another unmade road reserve partly fenced on both sides. This reserve was inspected in 1984 and it was easily put into our scheme of things being unmade with very good views over the hills and ranges both to the east and west, and north over a part of the Mt Crawford Forest. I continued with the survey of the Trail until we reached the Bethany Reserve just at the bottom of the Barossa Range where Tanunda Creek comes out of the hills. This part of the ranges was new to me and I was immediately impressed. It was about September time, and as we came off Rifle Range Road we saw the sight of a lifetime. The hills had had some rain and were

Singing… – maybe not, but we did do plenty of walking in the rain, particularly here, near Melrose

greening up, on the valley floor 300 metres below, the vines were just beginning to show their first hint of green, contrasting with rectangles of deep chocolate of newly turned paddocks and here and there the first new grasses of spring were struggling for recognition.

I went in to a prearranged meeting with the District Council and told them of our plans of which they were already familiar, got the OK for what we wanted to do, plus the names of the adjoining owners on the unfenced side of the reserves. These were later contacted and all gave a positive reply, but as it turned out we did not get back on to that part of the job until 1987. This was just after the 'Friends of the Heysen Trail' had been formed and were getting themselves organized into an effective work force. The first project that they undertook unsupervised was to mark the Trail between the Mt Crawford and Kaiserstuhl Forest reserves. This was quite a straight forward job and I was surprised to get a phone call during the morning from Neville Southgate, the second president of the "Friends" in which he told me that having arrived at the start of the reserve, they had been bailed up by the adjoining land owner who had recently built a house adjacent to the reserves and was claiming that it was no longer open to the public. They said they feared that walkers would look in their bedroom window, steal their children, the water from their tanks etc. etc. I checked with the District Council and the Surveyor Generals Department and they confirmed that the road was still crown land and therefore open to the public. I offered the complaining landowners many compromises but none were considered. I went ahead and had the trail marked and so began a long running battle The battle was destined to go on for the rest of the time that I worked for the S.A. Government and for all I know it may still be going on. In the few situations like this that did occur land owner's tactics were wide and various. Some would summons me to a meeting, where they would then harangue me, usually adopting aggressive poses, always unpleasant, always with veiled threats. Others used the tactic of bailing up walkers as they went along the trail, putting their case to them, then if they got the sort of answer they wanted, they would phone me telling me that even walkers did not agree with the Trail going past their property. On a number of occasions these calls finished with some observation regarding fat cat public servants deliberately sending walkers past their land.

Some objectors to the Trail development had the issue put on the agenda at the District Council meeting always taking care to have the numbers stacked against me. One owner wrote to the newspapers complaining about the Heysen Trail and me, but this had the reverse action as some of their neighbours wrote back to the paper to defend the trail and its users. One landowner went to the Ombudsman, not only did they lose there, they also accused the Ombudsman's officer, quite wrongly of leaving gates open and causing cattle to stray onto the road. Some took their case to the Minister of Recreation and Sport, John Oswald who had a meeting with them at Parliament House at which I was present. Out of all of this the message for them and the rest of us was clear. No individual can have the exclusive use of public land.

Waymarkers, huts, camps & bridges

In the beginning there were paint marks on rocks and trees, put there by the Adelaide Bush Walkers during the 1960s. This was a fairly inexpensive way of marking trails and if you had the key to the colour coding it was quite effective. It also had the advantage of being long lasting and low maintenance. It looked awful of course and was a miserable job for the poor wretch that scored the task.

I had experienced just one week of painting waymarkers insitu in the bush between Mt Falkland and the Wilcolo Track. This was before such modern inventions as the spray can, and water-based paints and so had some inherent problems. We carried two converted bean tins or similar, one containing bright orange Dulux and a second with turps plus brushes. Armed with these we set off in the cool clear air of a Flinders morning all boding well. We went off at a leisurely pace; what could be better, fine weather, the Flinders, peace and solitude, a cool breeze in the face, all this at $18 an hour. The first few markers were easily coated, we even argued whose turn it was to do the brush work. The task took on special significance, we were not simple artisans but craftsmen. We were the brushmen of the bush and compared ourselves with Hart, Absalom and Namatjira but as time passed the glamour of our task wore off. The day began to warm up , the turps now evaporated, heady acrid fumes were always with us, the paint thickened and slowly advanced up the brush handle defying all natural laws, including gravity.

This paint was of a particularly cunning type. It crept up the inside of the can then ran down the outside when we were not looking, ambushed our fingers and once having established a bridgehead there it slowly advanced over our hands. We always put too much paint on the brush – what else are you supposed to do. The brush has to be submersed in the paint or there would be no point to the exercise.

Now I can see the old hands winking at each other, nodding the heads and drawing the breath over their teeth in the way that the knowing do. Well of course I know that you are supposed to wipe off the excess liquid on the side of the can and this works well in theory, but in practice its a failure. The thing that the experts don't seem to understand is that a paint brush is flat and straight sided whereas a baked bean can is round and this always meant that there was more orange fire on the brush than strictly needed. This excess either stayed on the brush until the brush was applied to the waymarker whereupon it sallied forth down the post like wayward lava going for a day out in Pompeii, or leapt to the ground and freedom, or made a frontal assault on our hands, wrists or forearms or any other part of our bodies unwittingly exposed.

The result of our efforts were most unsatisfactory. By the end of the week we had applied more paint to the Flinders Ranges than to the waymarkers and despite rigorous scrubbing each night at the end of the job both Martin and myself appeared to be wearing long Orange Fire evening gloves. This did not impress the other diners at the Wilpena Chalet one bit.

The NFC subcontracted the marking of their Trails, a network of footpaths planned to extend throughout the Mt Lofty Ranges from the Barossa south to the Fleurieu Peninsula, to a certain Edmund Lovegrove, a man of singular personality who was still at university at the age of 48 years. Ted as he was known, disliked paint splodges on rocks as much as I did and devised his system based on a 6 inch equilateral triangle. This was made from 18 gauge galvanized sheet painted yellow and with 3 3/8th holes punched in it towards the corners. These markers were to be nailed onto fence posts and trees. Where there were no suitable posts or trees they were replaced with 2 inch galvanized iron water pipe the top 6 inches painted yellow. There was also a logo which consisted of two black bootprints on a yellow ground, screen printed on the same material as the waymarker, 6 x 6inches in size. There were also signs informing walkers of whose land they were about to enter.

As this system of trails was designed to be a network of paths and rights of way, each junction of trails was marked with a number on the map and on the ground a white 2" disc bore the number of the junction. Below this further discs with triangles pointing to other junctions, the product of Lovegrove's diagramatical mind.

The system was sound in theory and did in practice work tolerably well, with some problems but with its difficulties ironed out was pretty much the system that was used on the Heysen Trail.

One of the major problems was that putting signs on trees made a mess of the tree even if the triangle was put up in a square and workman like fashion which it rarely ever was. It was always our intention to get the marker as high up a tree as we could. This posed no difficulty if we were working out of our trusty Landcruiser or within easy reach of it but this was not usually the case and so we were often obliged to nail the triangle to the tree at full stretch standing on tip toe.

This combined with the choice of 3 inch galvanized roofing clouts was a sure recipe for disaster. We would hold the marker up with one hand, arm at full stretch, then somehow with the other push the nail through the hole into the bark of the gum, then with the waymarker temporarily in place we would strive to hammer the nail home. This was where the trouble began. It took about ten good hearty blows of the hammer to drive the 3 inch nail home but being inept with this sort of tool and being in such at awkward position, only about one blow in three ever hit the nail on the head the others either smashing into the triangle or the unfortunate eucalyptus. The result of all this was that the nice new bright yellow marker looked as though it was the victim of the Basingstoke axe murderer. Most of the paint had been knocked off, the galvanized coating stripped away and the clean crisp lines of the triangle bludgeoned into a piece of scrap metal, so degraded that not even Simsmetal would have found a use for it.

Lovegrove and I did get better at it over time but as we used a lot of volunteers most waymarkers suffered the same fate

This was not the end of the story, many eucalypts rejected the marker by growing a mass of material behind the sign and forcing it off the trunk, others exuded a thick dark sap over the triangle making it useless, some however can still be found clinging desperately to the occasional post and dead tree.

The junction posts were never popular as I don't believe most people think in the abstract too well. I could never understand why it was more efficient to call the junction say B57 and have markers pointing the way to B10 or A17. I mean these places all had names so what was wrong with calling the junction Wilson's Bog and have markers indicating the way to Holland Creek or Pages Flat.?

The stile was very popular

The other NFC Lovegrovian innovation was the stile introduced to overcome the problem of walkers leaving gates open.

The Lovegrove design was a superior one manufactured from mild steel tube and 1.1/2 inch strip. It was simply a ladder about 14 feet long with 6 rungs, bent in two forming a sort of step ladder with 3 rungs on each side. At the bottom of each end was welded the steel strip. To erect the stile, a trench was dug the length of the steel strip, 6 inches x 12 inches deep, on either side of the fence to be crossed, the stile was then put in place and the trench filled with assorted rocks, earth and packed down.

This worked well for the most part but had one serious fault in that the steel used was not galvanized and the legs of the stile sometimes rusted through at the base. On more than one occasion a heavily laden backpacker on climbing one of these stiles has pulled himself up to the top rung only to find himself launched backwards

into space still clutching the top of the stile. The problem with this particular design was that it was easy to remove in one piece and they could be put to many a good use down on the farm. On one occasion I found that an Adelaide Hills landowner would take our stile and re-erect it over his fence so that it was convenient for him and his family to get on to the Trail as they all enjoyed a walk. Another time I strolled past a farmyard when something caught my eye, the shape was familiar but for a moment went unrecognized, then it dawned on me. Up against the diesel tank stand was a ladder, one of my stiles straightened out and wired to the top of the tank. Nevertheless some of these old metal stiles can still be seen 25 years later.

Out of all of this there slowly evolved the system of markers in use today. The concept of logo and the triangle as a waymarker still remain and so does the 'snow pole'. I put a stop to the use of trees as soon as I took charge of the project.

It was at this time that the Woods and Forest Dept. began offering permapine fencing posts as an alternative to the old creosote ones that were such a rotten sticky mess to handle. At 4 inch diameter and cut to length they suited us perfectly. We cut one end of each post to a chiseled point with two flat faces cut at 60 degrees, these two flats were painted white which could be seen from a fair distance, then a waymarker was mounted on the flat, although this was quickly superseded when we found that we could rout the triangle into the flat and then fill it with paint. The posts were than set in the ground using a post hole digger. These worked very well and some of the early ones are still working today.

However the pine post proved unworkable in the Flinders Ranges, the digging of the post holes taking far too long even when using power post hole diggers. So, for these stretches of rocky country we went back to the old snow post idea, using a fencing star dropper sprayed colorbond green and with the top 6 inches painted orange fire.

At first we used standard fencing droppers but later had them made to our own specification, that's to say a more appropriate length, no wire holes or slots and completely coated in hot dip galvanize These could be driven into almost any sort of ground with a thumper or sledge hammer. The direction was given by a 6 inch x 1 inch metal strip covered in red vinyl and with the logo silk screened onto it The star dropper was later replaced by a lightweight tubular picket.

In 1988 the Woods and Forest Department began producing 4x4 inch square posts and these were adopted and the logo was redesigned. The logos were made narrower to fit flush on the post so that no corners or edges were protruding and longer so that an area of the logo was left blank This was done to accommodate a self adhesive waymarker, and so the old steel triangle was done away with.

The south wall of Wilpena Pound

We developed a great liking for permapine and were soon using it for making stiles These were of the old European type that had been in use for hundreds of years, we also used permapine to make board walks through sand dunes and a raised walkway through Brady's Gully, a notorious bog and a massive staircase up the Kaolin Cliffs on Willochra Creek.

I remember during the early days of the Trail being highly amused when a lady phoned me to inquire if I could provide her with a map showing the locations of the huts along the Heysen Trail. I jokingly told her that with the sort of funding we received to build the Trail we had difficulty in buying a new wheelbarrow. The lady then told me of her experiences overseas where she had avoided carrying a heavy pack because there were huts and Hostels a day's walk apart along the paths. This was a very desirable feature of the Trails of course, but the cost was simply beyond our resources. The best we could do was to make sure that the path went close to existing YHA hostels, and this we did. I did not seriously contemplate the provision of accommodation beyond the development of fairly basic camp sites. We used whatever existing facilities were available and the Woods and Forest Department and National Parks and Wildlife Service developed camping areas placed close to the Heysen Trail when appropriate. They were usually constructed around an existing building or ruin that was then partly restored to provide a roof area that would in turn supply runoff water to a tank and also cover a basic cooking area. This would be augmented with a deep hole toilet.

Apart from this, walkers had to make their own arrangements. I came into the office after a field trip one morning during 1988 to be told that the day before someone had been looking for me regarding the building of a hut in the Flinders Ranges. This was a complete mystery to me although everyone in the office seemed to think that I was behind it. A few days later the mystery was cleared up. Neville Southgate and Paul Nicholas caught up with me to explain. These two blokes were from the Uniting Church Wright Court Day Centre, a centre that ran programs for homeless men. Paul Nicholas as well as being a welfare worker was a stonemason. He had teamed up with a retired builder Keith Hall and Greg Lowe to form a group

This group, working under the banner 'A hand up not a hand out', was to be used to give homeless men the opportunity to do some useful work, earn some wages and to learn a variety of useful skills, with the additional advantage of being located in remote areas away from some of the causes of their problems. They had got a grant to restore Mayo's Cottage which was on a bluff overlooking both Wonoka and Mernmerna Creeks at the eastern end of Mayo Gorge, a truly magnificent setting, and only a stone's throw from the Heysen Trail.

The last time I had seen the ruin it was barely recognizable from the surrounding gibber and now I was looking at a photograph of it much the same as it had been a century before. It was truly an amazing piece of restoration work. The inside was fitted out for walkers rather than a family, with bunks, open fire place and cooking facilities. This was to prove a very welcome sight for walkers after a long trip through the Flinders. These huts were never locked and there was no way of booking them. I was often asked how many walkers they could sleep and what would happen if a group of hikers arrived to find the hut full?

Looking south from Blacks Gap

The answer we always gave was this. "The hut is designed to sleep 10 people in comfort, 20 in discomfort and 40 in abject poverty."

The building of Mayo Hut set our minds off on a new train of thought. If huts could be built as part of a training scheme for home-less people providing them with an opportunity for a new start, and as a result of this a series of heritage rural buildings were restored and these used to augment the tourism and recreation opportunities, we would have a very sound argument for getting funding for a hut construction program.

We decided that the shortest day's walk worth doing would be 15km and the longest that an ordinary walker would undertake would be about 25km. Using this formula we calculated that we would need about 75 Huts along the Trail, with the one already built and the five existing YHA Hostels; this left us to find the funding for just 69.

The following year we got funding to construct a hut at Crystal Brook in Bowman Park, but now the bureaucrats wanted to get in on the act. I was instructed that all future building work must be carried out under the supervision and control of the Public Building Department, known from here on as the PBD.

There was no old building suitable for restoration and so we were forced to build a new one. What we wanted was something along the lines of an outstation or cattlemen's hut, I put this to the experts who nodded sagely, yes, they knew just what we wanted, and then went off and totally ignored our needs; did what they wanted. A very nice structure quite inappropriate for our use and at twice the cost. During the construction I visited the site and spoke to the builder and then told the person from the PBD what I thought was wrong. On my return to the office I was summoned before my supervisor and told

that I was not the Recreation and Sport PBD liaison officer and to keep out of it in the future. Despite this setback the following year we took back the initiative and got on with the hut building program in the way it should have been done, using the supervisors, craftsmen and men from the Wright Court Day Centre and restoring rural buildings.

In this ham fisted amateur way we added between us, 14 huts to the infrastructure of the Heysen Trail all completed on time and under budget. These included; an 1880's timber cutter's cottage, 1900 forester's home, 1920 gun club , 1884 school, 1930 railway station, and an 1890 farm house to name a few.

The Federal Government came good with a grant of $100,000 to add to a lesser amount from the South Australian Government. In addition to this, C.S.R Softwoods donated timber and Mintaro Slate gave us the free run of its seconds store

we used whatever we could to place our markers

One of the unexpected spin-offs of the scheme was the increased interest of rural communities in the Heysen Trail.

They were very interested in their District's heritage buildings and of course we were the first Government Department to do anything to preserve them. We had formal openings of the Huts, usually a barbecue, and the locals always turned out in droves to have look at the restored building. They also came out to the site during construction and took a great interest in the men, bringing gifts of food and the offer of hot showers in town.

In 1989 the Wright Court Centre was presented with a State Recreation Award at a ceremony at the Hilton Hotel. All the men were there immaculately turned out in black tie and dinner jackets. Where the suits came from I thought it best not to ask. There is still a long way to go but the hut building program seems to have fallen by the wayside.

We built many bridges over the life of the Trail, at first they were, inventive. Money was short and we had to make do with whatever we could scrounge. So our first efforts tended to be largely made out of fencing wire and whatever wood we could get hold of and of course black baling twine.

Strangely enough these worked quite well, no one was ever hurt by one and they certainly prevented walkers having to attempt fording of creeks in spate, something that accounts for the life of many walkers and climbers each year. The biggest problem was that they needed very high levels of maintenance and were prone to be damaged during flash flooding.

The Onkaparinga River provided our biggest challenges. Over the years several attempts were made to bridge the stream but flash floods always beat them.

One of the most ambitious was undertaken not by the Government but by the Baptist Church. The Baptist Church has a camp on the north bank of the river and each year holds a series of camps for less able bodied children most of whom are confined to wheel chairs. Despite being in wheelchairs the kids do some amazing things, but there was no way that could cross the Onkaparinga. This of course denied them access to all of the country to the south of the river.

The camp was run at this time by Fred Groom and his wife, a couple known for their resource and initiatives. Fred determined to build a bridge that could accommodate a wheelchair and set about putting a team of supporters together to undertake the project.

With acquisition of a disused crane cable, a donation of timber and sundry other materials, a very sturdy bridge was soon spanning the stream, though with the irregular flooding of the river the bridge's lifespan was limited. Sometime after this it was decided to call in the experts and have a proper engineering job done. $35,000 later a splendid suspension bridge leapt across the divide constructed above the 100 year flood mark. It was to be called the Warren Bonython bridge and was opened by him at a public function in February 1990. Just two months later a flash flood came roaring down the valley and the bridge has not been seen since, although there was an uncon-firmed report that it had been seen cruising in Backstairs Passage.

Lost Walkers

We found ourselves on our way back to the Flinders on yet another unscheduled visit. A party of walkers had decided to walk the Heysen Trail from Yannyanna Hut to Wilpena in a day, a distance of about 20km. To a reasonably fit group this would not be a big ask, particularly if an early start was made. Well it now seemed that this party was not fit, nor did it get an early start. They were way behind schedule when mother nature decided to intervene as she is often wont to do when the unknowing flout the rules.

It does not rain often in the Ranges but when it does nature puts on a fine show - the heavens open, roads become impassable, creeks break their banks, and visibility is greatly reduced. This all happened as our valiant walkers struggled though the ABC Range with night coming on. A short journey through some very tortured and incised hills, and so it was past night fall when they emerged on to the eastern bank of Wilcolo Creek only to find its usually dry stony bed the host to a roaring torrent dashing off to join Bunyeroo Creek, bearing with it trees and bushes in great number.

The group fortunately had the sense not to attempt to cross and instead worked their way upstream until either they arrived at a safe crossing or the torrent had begun to subside, or a combination of both so that they were able to cross and join the Wilcolo Trail.

By now it was late, way past the time that they were expected at Wilpena and they still had some very difficult country to traverse. There was still every prospect of more rain so the walkers decided to walk back to Bunyeroo following the Wilcolo Track. Meanwhile back at the Rangers H.Q. the non-arrival of the walkers had been reported and a search was under way and was soon successful in finding the group on the Wilcolo Track not far from where they had crossed the creek. Now the recriminations. The walkers were suitability embarrassed and blamed their failings on the marking of the Heysen Trail. Hence our presence in the Ranges. This sort of reaction was not unusual. It was all too easy to blame the Trail when your own inexperience was at fault. Although we had several instances of this sort of thing they could not be substantiated. Any report of a walker in trouble always brought us to our feet. One I remember very well went like this:

'A group of young walkers are overdue on a walking trip. All of the teenagers are over 21'!.

Hughes Gap to Mt Remarkable

Jack Slater was now the Minister of Rec. and Sport. I liked Jack and we got on well. He had been the General Secretary of the Boot Makers Union for almost 30 years and it was sometimes said by the unknowing that he had got his place in the Ministry as reward for his service to the Labor Party and would simply sit out his term until it was time to collect his pension., Well I saw a much different side to Jack. He often came into the office without his minders, remembered names and projects and was always encouraging. He could be tough when needed and had on more than one occasion showed he could get things done and done quickly. I saw Jack years after he had left Government, sitting outside the Grasshopper Roadhouse at Tarlee having coffee. Not having seen him for many years I approached hesitantly but Jack looked up and saw me "Good day Terry. How's the Heysen Trail going?" He introduced me to his companion and we had a long chat, Jack was off to the Clare races for the weekend. Good on him.

At this time there was a lot of Federal funding about for employment programs, known this time around as Commonwealth Employment Program, or C.E P. better known to us as CEPTIC and I decided that we should try for a share of it. The scheme this time was to favour employment in the rural areas, which were particularly depressed at the time. As our next section of the Trail was to be from Crystal Brook to Mt Brown I felt that we had a more than equal chance. However before I could get to grips with the submission, one of my colleagues from another section casually asked me how I felt about John Riggs of the Woods and Forests Dept. taking over the Heysen Trail project. As you may well imagine I was very disturbed, I had now given this project my all over the last eight years had done most of the hard work and felt a strong sense of ownership. I also knew John Riggs quite well as he had been my first point of contact during the negotiations to route the Trail through Forest reserves. I had always thought of him as an honest and straightforward bloke. I made an urgent call to John and arranged to meet him. We met at the Tinsmiths building the next day. I was still very annoyed at the way the proposal had come to me but John Riggs soon calmed the situation down with his explanation of the proposal. The Crystal Brook section of the Trail would largely pass through the Wirrabara and Mt Remarkable forest reserves. The Woods and Forest Dept. already had an existing infrastructure in the area, H.Q. workshop, transport supervision, admin. and financial services. The proposal would be that

Recreation would retain the overall control of the design of the Trail, negotiate the right of way and the overall supervision of the construction of the path with Woods and Forests providing the day to day supervision of the works and be the receiver of the grant money and control the finances including the responsibility for the payment of wages. This arrangement had the advantages that more of the grant funds could be put into employing people from the local district rather than bring staff up from the city and having to pay overnight expenses and meal allowances. The scheme worked well. The three people selected for the job proved to be hard workers, very hard workers. The section of Trail that they were contracted to make and mark was through the Wirrabara Forest then over Mt Remarkable and down to the Spring Gully mine. This was a particularly steep and rugged part of the Trail. Not only was it steep country but also very rocky with hardly any top soil. This made the installation of the way markers extremely arduous. We had struggled for years to develop a waymarker that was satisfactory, our preferred model at this time was a metre length of permapine post 4 inches in diameter with about one foot cut off at an angle of 60 degrees and a triangle routed into this flat. The flat was then painted brown with the triangle in orange fire. This type of post had proved to be the best in most ways with the exception of bush fire when it seemed to evaporate leaving no trace. The one drawback was that it had to be placed into an 18 inch post hole and with 8 markers to the kilometre and 40 kilometre to mark that meant making over 300 post holes almost all of which had to be cut through hard shale.

The way from the summit of Mt Remarkable to Spring Gully followed a steeply undulating fire access trail and I ordered that the path should leave the access trail wherever practical and contour along the east flank of the range. This deviation made life much harder for the trail makers as the ground was strewn with slabs of loose rock all of which had to be cleared from the footway. It must have been extremely hard work and went on for months but they never shirked and kept going week after week. The Trail was complete by the end of November and I planned to have it open at the beginning of the walking season, but in February a terrific wild fire swept through the Ranges up over Mt Remarkable and almost all of the way to Wilmington, totally destroying not only the work that our Woods and Forest people had done but also all the work done by ourselves and the considerable efforts of the Friends of the Heysen Trail. Those of us who had seen the aftermath of bush fire could not recall any fire that had such devastating results. Over a third of the work done over the last six months was gone and with only two months to go before the scheduled opening which had been well publicized and a good number of maps sold in advance.

The thought of hundreds of disgruntled walkers milling about the forest expecting to find a clearly marked trail was an unhappy one, a situation that did not appeal. George Belchev then the Executive Officer of Recreation and Sport, a man who supported the development of the Trails, somehow managed to find some additional funding and the clarion call went out to the Friends of the Heysen Trail for help. Thelma Andersen was the executive officer of the 'Friends' at the time. Thelma saw to it that the call was answered. Over the next few weeks we were able to keep a workforce in the field seven days a week 10 hours a day, with Andrew, Martin and myself working during the week with the few volunteers who could get time off and supervising the bulk of volunteers who came up in a rented 30 seater bus with some local residents, in this way we were able to open the Trail just one month late.

The arrangement with the volunteers was that they gave their time freely to the development of the Trail but should not be out of pocket. Therefore I organised funding to cover cost of accommodation, pub, caravan park or camp site, transport, and meals in whatever way appropriate, the point being that each volunteer came at some cost to the Trail's budget, which at this time was well funded but there was no fat, so every dollar had to be made to work. Our volunteers always worked hard and we got good value out of them but there were exceptions to this. One of these I remember very well. It was 11 o'clock on a Saturday morning when one of our senior members came and asked me if I could organize to take his wife back to Wilmington as she was unwell, and I did so without hesitation. Being concerned about the woman's health I inquired as to her condition. "Well" she said "I am not too good. I have just had a pace maker fitted and only came out of hospital 2 days ago." I asked if she thought it was entirely appropriate that she should come on an exercise such as this. She said she had thought it would make a nice change. A similar instance occurred later when we were working on the Trail nearer Quorn and staying at the Criterion Hotel. The bus arrived at the pub on Sunday night bringing with it a fresh batch of trailwrights. They were mostly old hands with a couple of new chums, one of whom was a tall willowy and rather decorative young women of about 30 summers called Jane. As the average age of our group was about 83 she was quite a star and the centre of attraction. The main task of the week was to mark the way over a very steep elevated ridge well covered with scrub. It would only take two or three volunteers to do the marking while the rest of us back packed the waymarkers up to the ridge top. This we did throughout the Monday. The next morning we met for breakfast, Jane did not appear. I suggested to Tom, her self appointed minder, that he should get her up as I was not prepared to wait for anyone. Tom then told us that she had woken him at 3 am and persuaded him to take her to Port Augusta so that she could get the 8 o'clock bus to Adelaide and this he had done. Just what the lady thought we were paying her travel and accommodation expenses for I can't imagine.

Mt Rrmarkable to Quorn

Negotiating the course of the Trail through the Wilmington Melrose district was certainly the most difficult and painful of all the negotiations that I went through. I have already described the way in which public meetings were conducted in an earlier chapter.

The meetings here were pretty much par for the course. The main problem seemed to be that the area was dominated by a few heavies who did most of talking at the meetings. I had not at that time encountered such personal hostility nor did I ever again. I wrote to all the landowners who might be involved and received not one single reply. Melrose could be in my view the most scenic village in the Flinders Ranges yet it is entirely spoilt mainly by a line of the most ugly and inappropriately sited Stobie poles, aided and abetted in the ruination of the place, is one of the pubs, a fine stone building painted a lurid sickly pale green and an enormous Toyota sign that hangs outside the garage competing with all the other visual pollution for some sort of garbage grand prix. I held a series of meetings in the district and these were always dominated by an aggressive clique. Until I resorted to the rather low trick of seeding a meeting with a bus load of supporters of the Heysen Trail with such notables as Warren Bonython, Thelma Anderson and Andrew Eastick, a sheep farmer from the southeast, all of whom were prepared to go in hard, and after this meeting I began to get somewhere. The Council formed a local Heysen Trail Development committee to which I agreed. Their offering after several weeks was, follow a dirt road from the Wirrabra Forest then through the Mt Remarkable Conservation Park then over another back road to Quorn, all this despite there being a series of unmade road reserves most of the way. This account of a negotiation will illustrate what I was up against. I explained to a group of graziers that I only intended to use unmade public roads. "No" they said "you can't identify them" so they offered to let me use only roads that had one side fenced. To this I agree, much to their surprise, they consult. "No sorry, what we meant was reserves that are fenced on both sides." "OK" says I, collective jaws drop, "um, um err um" new condition coming up "what we mean is that you can have your trail on reserves that are fenced on both sides only if they are not used by the local farmers" I went home. Another instance, I had to find a way of connecting the Willowie Forest, now part of the Mt Remarkable Conservation Park to the Alligator Gorge National Park. These two great areas of land were divided by a piece of freehold property approximately 2.5km in width. If I could not negotiate a way over this then the alternative was to take the way out of the Range then on a 15km road bash to Horrocks Pass. My investigations found an old reserve in just the place that we needed it. I approached the landowner of the adjoining property. "No it can't be, the road has disappeared long ago." I point out that one of the fences is still intact. "Yes" he agrees "but which one, get it wrong and your trail will be trespassing." I explain that I can tell by the fence's relationship to an adjoining double fence line. "I won't accept that from you. Get a survey done". He is astute enough to know that funding is not available in sufficient quantities for a survey. I go to the Lands Dept. They do not have funding either but do provide me with a copy of the original title and plan, which is sent off to the landowner who does not reply. Then we receive an offer of help, from the Institute of Surveyors. They will survey one end of the reserve if we can pay the members' petrol cost. This we happily accept and the part survey is carried out. I make one final bid to get the landowner on side and we meet in Wilmington but now he tells me that the roads in country areas were never intended to be used by the public but only to give neighbours access through adjoining properties. Well you have to give the bloke top marks for tenacity but I had had it and left him. The next day in the office I wrote to him telling him that I would be marking the path and give details of time and place and invited him to take the appropriate action. On the appointed date I set off to the start of the reserve with a group from the 'friends' one of whom was Jamie Shephard. I arrived at the beginning of the reserve before the others who were putting in waymarkers as they advanced up the creek. There I found, not the owner but his two sons. I introduced myself and they invited me to leave which I declined to do. All the old arguments were trotted out but I could detect a lack of conviction. They obviously had little enthusiasm for the game and I was quite sure that the old man had not told them the whole story. Just then Jamie Shephard arrived, immaculately turned out, as always, looking like a cross between Sir Edmund Hilary and Biggles. He strode straight up to the group, came to attention, leaned slightly forward, clicked his heels, thrust his hand forward "splendid morning eh chaps?" The spell was broken and the owner's sons made a dignified strategic withdrawal. W.E. Johns would have been proud.

It is odd how a small, seemingly insignificant action can have quite profound effects. I have seen it many times.

On one occasion I was speaking to a rather reluctant farmer, a man by the name of Featherstonehaugh which he pronounced Feather-stone-hore, now I am a student of history, the only subject that I was anywhere near good at in school, much to the dismay of my parents. I remembered that Featherstonehaugh is one of those names that came over to Britain with the conqueror, names like Mainwhereing pronounced Mannering or Beauchamps but said as Beecham and Featherstonehaugh pronounced Fanshaw. I told the landowner this story adding that I thought he was probably a direct descendant of one of the old Norman Lords. He quite changed his attitude after that and we got on very well. Incidentally I know all this because the name Lavender comes down to me from the Norman invaders, the name though is anything but lordly, meaning cleaner of loos although the number of toilets they had in those days I should think that they were about as busy as an assistant snow plough operator in Trinidad, which is probably where I get my preference for idleness, preferring to go walking than working.

This part of the path went through Horrocks Pass. The Pass is named after John Ainsworth Horrocks who passed that way whilst searching for good grazing land west of the Flinders Ranges. Poor old John was out of luck. One day he happened to drop his gun which he kept loaded, and on hitting the ground it discharged and wounded him very badly in the leg. The poor fellow must have suffered appallingly. With no analgesic the journey back to Penwortham must surely have been a nightmare. Poor old John did make it back but died a short time later from his wound. There is a rather unpleasant obelisk of stone in the pass as a memorial to him. I find the wording on the brass plague a bit objectionable it says something to the effect that Horrocks discovered the pass in the company of a 'native'. I would think the 'native' probably knew the pass was there for years.

There is a wonderful high ridge running just about due north up to Mt Brown then down into Waukarie Creek approximately 6km east of Woolshed Flat. A perfect walk; wild, isolated elevated reaching over 3,000 ft on the summit of Mt Brown. The distance between Horrocks Pass and Woodshed flat was over 40km. I was determined that this ridge should be part of the Trail. My investigations found a reserve running all the way to the top of Mt Brown. The first 30km was a 2 chain reserve, that is to say forty four yards or the length of two cricket pitches. This is fairly unusual. Almost all of the reserve was fenced on one side and quite obvious. Then, there was a 1 chain section that was not so easy to follow. The final section of the reserve was not only unfenced but was over a 5 chain reserve originally set aside to provide access to the Trig Point on the summit of Mt Brown. There was about 4km of the reserve without a fence or survey peg and to make the thing much worse the reserve twisted and turned before passing into the Mt Brown Forest. There was no chance of us being able to mark the Trail with any degree of accuracy. As we were constantly under scrutiny by the landowners we could take no chances. I got a quote for the cost of a survey, the price $35,000. This seemed outrageous but I was told that the nearest bench mark was some distance from the reserve and there was no vehicular access to anywhere near the site. Even so we were stunned by the estimate. There was no way the funding could be found from the Deparments budget. This news soon spread throughout the district and things calmed down in the belief that the route from Horrocks Pass to Mt Brown would be abandoned.

4-Wheel Drives

The course of our work took us into some very remote and difficult country, often steep and inaccessible, through creeks, across boggy back tracks and deep sandy bush. If it had not been for a series of Toyota Landcruisers I think we might be there still. Everyone has a 4-WD story and here is one of mine

During the mid 1970's I was in the company of Hugh Morgan, another refugee from the old NFC. We had been working on a trail in the Para Wirra National Park, it was one of those wet winters and we had spent most of the day getting damper and colder, but it was a job that had to be finished so we worked on until about 5:30pm and then returned to the City, deciding to spurn the gravel road that would take us to One Tree Hill and instead take a short cut south of Humbug Scrub, east along a little used track. This would cut the agony of hunger and dripping clothes by at least 20 minutes. It was true that the area was saturated and there was some risk but we rationalized we had a Toyota Landcruiser, one of the best off road vehicles.

It was also true that the light was going, but we were experienced. Morgan had driven over half Africa in search of depression Gold during the 1930's and I had learned my skills during my time working for the Outward Bound Trust in the less exotic location of Dartmoor. Yes we were equal to it and the thought of getting to the pub 20 minutes early was an added bonus. We set off, myself behind the wheel and Morgan acting as pilot. The deeper we drew into the forest the stronger came the rain, by now stair rods slashing the headlight beam and we were soon in a very small yellow world of our own, bound by a solid wall of blackness. Nevertheless we made good progress; we stopped a couple of times while Hugh checked the ground, kicking and stamping in a most impressive way, then with him giving his approval we continued on our way. Just when we reckoned the worst was over we reached the low point of a shallow valley, the headwaters of Mack's Creek. The creek was flowing fairly fast, 18 inches or so deep and even in the jaundiced light it was obviously flowing over a good stony bed. Morgan climbed from the vehicle and soon reappeared in the circle of light to once again perform his strange musicless hornpipe, toe first, then the heel of his boot was applied to the bottom of the creek, first right foot then the left, he walked out of the light reappearing next to me in the Toyota, a shape-less, damp but quite heroic figure. We discussed tactics. It was agreed. Hugh being the eldest should drive, and I being the least experienced should take up a position on the far bank where I would wave my arms around in an inane meaningless fashion and although Hugh

would completely ignore me and I would be totally irrelevant to the task at hand it was felt that this would give me a sense of involvement. And so it was, Hugh at the wheel, knuckles white, weather-beaten face barely showing in the leprous glow behind the windscreen, clenched into a 'Wages of Fear' expression, edged the great machine forward, and I began my unrelated semaphore on the far bank. There was a great anti climax, Hugh piloted the Landcruiser over the creek and on to the far bank without difficulty. I climbed in beside the great man, "home please". We moved 2 feet and the whole damned thing sank up to its belly in the mud of the far bank, and so began the cold wet job of digging the 4-wheel out, but we were experienced men, out of Africa, out of Dartmoor. What was this to us, a mere bagatelle? We dug, we jacked, we filled, we watched the bloody thing, jack, fill and all, sink deeper into the slough of despond. After hours of work we had expended all our energy, all our initiative.

We had gained a few feet of mud, we knew how the troops must have felt on Flanders field. We gave up, and began the oh so long walk to the Ranger's house at Para Wirra wet, cold, hungry and tired but none of this occupied our minds as much as what would be our reception when we finally arrived at our destination. As we tramped the fluid miles a plan formed in my mind. Was this my doing?, was I

Looking east toward Logan Gap

driving when we bogged? I thought of a dozen reasons why I should not bear the responsibility and resolved that when we reached the Ranger's house I would, as we waited for the Ranger to awake from his slumbers and answer the door, slip into to the background, thereby allowing the rightful culprit to take the major portion of the blame. Morgan had the same dark thoughts and had developed a similar design. When we did reach salvation's door this resulted in some rather undignified shuffling but in the end it made little difference. It was not as late as we thought, the Ranger was still up and in need of a laugh which he got in good measure at the sight of us. We were home by midnight. As for the Toyota we retrieved it, with little difficulty the next day with the help of a local farmer and his tractor.

The Dog's Story

There is one thing that remains constant from farm to farm, and that is the working dogs. Go into a farm yard anywhere in South Australia and you will be met by a mob of dogs. The number of dogs at work on stations in this state must be huge. We all own dogs sometime during our lives but not like farm dogs. I used to feel quite sorry for working dogs but they don't seem to feel that way themselves, in fact they seem to be quite proud of the job they do and the skills that they have. I soon learnt that you will not endear yourself to a land owner if you stroke pet or talk to a working dog as this is considered to be a sign of feeble mindedness and will immediately expose you as, at best a city dweller or at worst a tourist which was pronounced terrorist in the country at that time. Country dogs should be ignored as they rarely bite, unlike town dogs.

On one occasion I went to see an owner near Lyndoch and was directed to a rather dark and dilapidated house high on a ridge. When I arrived and got out of the 4-wheel I found myself in what seemed to be a totally deserted farm; the only indication that it was inhabited was the presence of a large black dog, who on seeing me alight and leave the security of the vehicle, prepared for battle. Hackles up, teeth displayed, and head down, he gave his war cry and charged, running straight at me, I scrambled for the truck door, but before I could reach it the dog came to grief. It happened that he was moored to a ring set in the wall via a stout chain which with the dog having reached maximum speed in 0.52 of a second from a standing start now, reached the full extent of his fetters and was brought to a instant halt. At least his head did as the dog's body continued

"I think it's mud"

at full velocity, the feet overtaking the head until it was flipped by the force of its charge into the air and coming down on its side with a sickening crunch. Whether this dog had suffered a brain malfunction caused by its behaviour or whether it was born with some cerebral damage I never knew. It was certainly a few biscuits in the bowl short when I made its acquaintance, for it quickly got to its feet shook its head in the style of a prize fighter and backed up preparing for another assault. From then on whenever it saw me and judged I was within its exclusion zone it would launch a preemptive strike. It always misjudged the length of the chain and always ended up thumping into the stones of the yard.

Wilpena to Parachilna

In 1980, Ian Trestrail and I walked from Cape Jervis to Victor Harbor along the south coast of the Fleurieu Peninsula with the aim of assessing the possibilities for extending the Trail from Newlands Hill to the Cape.

We were impressed with the possibilities of the area and I hoped to be back on the Peninsula very soon. However not long after I returned to the office I was made aware that the Tourism Dept. was showing interest in the Trail's development. This soon manifested itself in a request that the next section of the Trail should be in the Flinders Ranges as this was to become the focus of a promotion in the coming years.

The Heysen Trail would greatly add to the accessibility of the area away from the usual tourist facilities and the few roads. I was disappointed at not being able to get on with the Trail on the Fleurieu Peninsula after all our recent exertions. However a high flying Government Department like Tourism giving us its support had to be taken seriously and we suggested that the Trail should be developed from Parachilna Gorge to the Wilpena Chalet, a distance of about 100km.

This would have the advantage of traversing the Flinders Ranges Wilderness Park and I believed then that only the owners of two pastoral leases would have to be negotiated with, and so the job could proceed fairly quickly. The problem of funding was as always with us but in recent times the Trails had been getting plenty of good publicity and so some additional funding was found.

I had worked in the Flinders during the early 1970s running Adventure camps based on Rawnsley Bluff, Clem Smith's place just south of the Pound and later as trainer and Board Member of the South Australian Bush and Mountain Walking Leadership Training Board, God what a mouthful, hereafter called the Bush Board.

Richard Massey and I had of course had a cursory look at the country in 1978 and so I began to prepare to negotiate the right of way. National Parks gave their usual enthusiastic support although they were well understaffed even at that time, so it would be a matter of doing the ground work, finding a way through the park from Aroona Ruin down to Wilpena, using where possible existing paths and of course picking the most scenic route consistent with cost of development and future maintenance costs. There was nothing difficult about that, just a lot of hard work, time, energy and logistics. The hard bit was going to be getting the two leaseholders on side.

Alpana Run was owned by John Henry and his family. The property bordered on the Parachilna to Blinman Road. Extending from the gorge pretty much all the way to the Blinman Hawker Road with the exception of the Blinman Cemetery and a small section of land just about mid way between the gorge and Blinman known as the Angorichina Hostel, which had up until recent years been a T.B hostel for returned soldiers. Neither of these sections would be of any concern to us.

I sent off the usual letters to the lease holders explaining our proposal and waited for a reaction. It came, but from an unexpected quarter. It was Tony Smith, Clem Smith's son who told me that he was now the proprietor of the old soldiers hostel and was running it as a school camp and hostel. He needed to increase his turnover and proposed that the Heysen Trail should go north through Alpana to Blinman pools then follow the Creek to his Hostel which of course would make Angorichina the focus of the northern end of the Trail and presumably increase his throughput of guests. I had not had a reply from either Alpana or Gum Creek but it was obviously being talked about in the district. Tony Smith ended his letter with an invitation to be his guest when next we visited the Blinman district.

This invitation troubled me a bit for I had fallen foul of Tony's father Clem some years before and as he had not yet extracted the promised retribution I concluded that where the son was the father would not be far away. My dispute with Clem had occurred in 1974 while I was running a mountain activities skills course based on Clem's Rawnsley Bluff Station immediately south of the southern wall of Wilpena Pound. It had been a particularly trying time for the staff due to massive rainstorms. It doesn't rain in the Flinders very often but when it does, conditions can become appalling. On this particular exercise we had two storms, one at the beginning of the camp which we recovered from, two weeks of beautiful Flinders winter weather and then on the last day another tropical storm. It happened just as we were getting some 30 clients ready for the trip to Adelaide, via 4-WD, out on to the western plain to catch the Ghan at Edeowie Railway station.

All this was accomplished despite flooded creeks, bogged vehicles and the train running two hours late. The plan was, having got the customers away, the staff would spend the rest of the day sorting out the mass of equipment we had used during the course, load the vehicles and trailers and be away early next morning.

As the final day drew into dismal evening it was found that some of the climbing equipment had been left at one of the outcamps on the base slopes of the Pound about 2km away.

I knew there was a track going quite near and so went and sought Clem's approval to take a vehicle up it. Well he really wasn't very happy about the use of the track due to the heavy rains but reluctantly agreed, however there was a proviso the track at one stage divided into two and I must not under any circumstances take the right-hand path. This was agreed and I began making my way up towards the Pound camp site. In the rain and dark I missed the Y junction and of course took the right-hand fork, got to the camp without difficulty but on the return trip bogged the 4-wheel, not too badly, and we soon had the thing dug out then repaired the track and went back to report. The house was dark and obviously the Smiths were in bed. I wasn't game to wake Clem then tell him about the damage to the track, and so went back to my damp sleeping bag. We left early the next morning without giving the events of the night before a thought. Back at the NFC work resumed and I heard nothing and presumed that the repairs to the track had been of the required standard and the episode was forgotten. It was not, Lavender had transgressed the code of the bush and retribution was required.

It seems that I was found guilty in my absence and this was relayed to me in a strange way. Some mates of mine were walking in the Arkaba area and had arranged to be picked up at Rawnsley at the end of the trip and as they were passing saw Clem and stopped to pass the time of day. At some stage in the conversation it transpired that they knew me. Clem gave them the grim message "Tell that bugger if he ever shows his face here again I'll bloody well fillet him." Whether the message had become enhanced in the various retellings before it was told to me I can't say but I had seen what Clem could do to a ewe with his filleting knife and neither business nor pleasure has taken me that way since.

I phoned Gordon McCullum and was well received; he had no problems with the Trail if it kept to the western side of his country which was on the eastern side of the Heysen Range and not much used for grazing. However Gordon was concerned that his neighbor John Henry who did have problems might be compromised if he gave permission without John being consulted and would not give me the go ahead until I had spoken to John Henry. He also added that he was getting too old to be involved in things like this and I should deal with his son Gordon in future. Next I phoned John Henry. This was a step back into the past, quite a pleasant one I should add, there was no direct dialing and I got through to the Blinman Exchange "Hello Blinman, can I have BK 27 Please" I inquired "You after John Henry?" I confirmed I was. "Sorry, he's gone fencing and won't be home for a couple of days." No recorded message, no Greensleeves, no invitation to press a further series of numbers, a real human being on the phone.

John seemed everywhere but at home, fencing, mustering, crutching, but in the end I found him. He was too busy to see me during the day and most nights of the week but eventually we made arrangements to meet. Two weeks later Martin and I were heading north to see Parks and Wildlife officers and landowners and finalise the route of the Trail through the Flinders Ranges Park at least.

We spent most of the week exploring the Park and found a splendid route from Aroona Ruin up to Red Hill Lookout and over the ABC Range, so called because it has more peaks than the alphabet has letters. Then south over Brachina Creek past Middlesight Water, on to Yanyana Hut then steeply down the head waters of Bunyeroo Creek, a second crossing of the ABC's along the Wilcolo Track, then up the side of the Pound and finally following the St. Mary's Peak Trail to Wilpena.

A wonderful walk with outstanding views of the heartland of the Flinders Ranges all around. The north wall of the Wilpena Pound in sight all the time and growing clearer with each step south.

Now for the hard bit, Parachilna Gorge to Aroona. We stayed one night at Angorichina meeting with the Smiths, no mention of Clem was made. They seemed to be putting a lot of hope in the Heysen Trail starting at their Hostel. Later over dinner they told me that they had met John Henry in an effort to persuade him to allow the Trail though his lease and into Blinman Pools. This made me feel that I was getting involved in some sort of local feud. I made it clear to the Smiths that I would be speaking to John Henry and as the leaseholder he would have to agree to any public use of the land, and although technically he may not have the power to prevent additional uses of the land, I could not in all conscience go against the will of the lessee.

What I did not tell them was that I had done some work on the legal aspects of this issue and there seemed no clear answer, not even the Pastoral Board could give a straight answer and had in fact told me that they had on six occasions sought legal opinions and each time had received different answers. There was little future for the Trail if the Department of Recreation got the reputation for riding roughshod over graziers.

A very dark and cold Flinders night it was, that night, as Martin and I drove out to Alpanna Run. The truck's high beam picked out the Henry's track in gold and very soon we saw the lights of the homestead shining through the night in the time honoured fashion of the bush. We passed half seen sheds, an array of mills and aerials and pulled up in front of the house, amid a flurry of working dogs who circled the Toyota muttering a mix of challenges, threats and welcomes.

A rectangle of cadmium appeared between two brightly lit windows and momentarily darkened as our host passed through the door.

Then John was guiding us into a fine large room with high ceilings. The introductions were made; John, his son and wife. John was shorter than me with a lean sparse frame that, like most cockies I met, looked hard and useful. He had an honest open face but with rather a

Mt Remarkable as seen from the summit of Mt Arden

sardonic look and I started to get the feeling that this was not going to be easy. John's wife was a good looking woman and like most of the country women I was to meet, dressed in the latest fashion well groomed in the same way, not the Ma and Pa Kettle you might expect.

Mrs Henry went off to bake fresh scones, we might be the enemy but would be treated with all the usual courtesies. The room was chilly but both John and his son were in shirtsleeves, sort of checked, thin black green and mustard lines on a white ground which seemed so favoured by farmers world wide. We were asked if the room was warm enough for us. We both replied, "Oh yes" in our deepest voices. The negotiations went well enough. John Henry had already foreseen the opportunity that tourism in the district might offer and so a walking trail through the property was a real possibility providing it went where John Henry directed, and this was definitely not via Blinman Pools. The Pools area being the property's best lambing paddock.

The route offered was to start in the Parachilna Gorge and go almost due south along an ancient mining track between the northern end of the ABC Range and the Heysen Range and could continue in the same way through Gum Creek Station all the way to Aroona Ruin. This would upset the Smiths as by following this route the Heysen Trail would start and finish some 10km distant from Angorichina and would not do much to increase their trade, but the offer was a fair one providing as it did an easy walk though some spectacular mountain scenery. It also had the advantage of having difficult but possible 4 wheel drive access which would keep development and maintenance costs down and walkers away from the station's activities.

The offer was conditional, first the neighbours had to agree, and the Third party liability had to be sorted out. Other issues such as fire bans, stiles, bridges and future maintenance costs had to be guaranteed by the Government. All this could be agreed to on the spot with the exception of the Third party liability.

I explained to John that Gum Creek had agreed so that was no problem, but then John put the first of the spanners in the works "What does Brian Reschke say about all this?" he asked me. This was a new name to me and my expression must have betrayed the fact.

"Mt Falkland Station, the Reschke's place" John added, "You have spoken with him I suppose?" "No, I said the Trail will only go over Alpana and Gum Creek" and produced the 1:50,000 topographic map to prove it.

It is a strange thing, graziers are such a pragmatic and resourceful lot yet I never met one who could master a topographic map.

I pointed to the various features on the map, blank faces, reading glasses fetched, still no recognition. Station map hurriedly sent for.

It's strange that trail makers are such a pragmatic and resourceful lot yet I never met one that could master a station owners map!. Neither one of us could convince the other and so I accepted that the Trail would cross the corner of Mt Falkland and agreed to see the owner the following day. That left the question of the Third party liability. This was a problem that was plaguing me and I had no satisfactory answer, just a lot of immature ideas, none of which would seem to solve the problem.

I explained to John who simply remarked that "You should not have started the Trail until these things were sorted out." Fair comment. So we left Alpana Run full of scones and coffee with the route of the Trail almost complete between Parachilna Gorge and Wilpena Pound and with some very large ifs.

If the lessees of Mt Falkland agreed to the Trail traversing their property and if I could get the liability issue solved.

We got back to Angorichina to find the place in darkness, the Smiths in bed and the generator switched off, and so spent a miserable time groping about in the dark on a very cold night. We breakfasted with Tony and his wife and broke the news over a fine plate of eggs and bacon with toast to follow and plenty of coffee. They were very upset, but the Trail could move on.

This was to be the last day of our field trip as we were now grandly calling them and had hoped for an early start for home. I wanted to get a look at John Henry's mine track and call on the Reschke's. So we crossed Parachilna Creek at a sharp bend in the road and spent the next two hours enveloped in the folds of the ABC and Heysen Ranges. Although the way passed through some of the most rugged range country our path was quite easy, an ideal combination for the Trail.

We headed west towards the main road looking to the north where we had been told we would see Mt Falkland Station, and were soon climbing up a track towards the homestead where we found a strange scene.

Standing on the gravel before the house stood one of those light-weight 4 WD vehicles that were so popular at that time with its bonnet up.

Moving around it were half a dozen people wandering about in a seemingly aimless fashion. I was loathe to interrupt, thinking this was some local tradition, a. dance or quadrille similar to the Morris men of my native Surrey or perhaps a form of greeting known only to the inhabitants of the Blinman District.

I suggested as much to Martin. He thought it much more likely that they had lost some part of the vehicle and were searching for it and so it proved to be. I approached and asked what was up and was told that an idiot son had decided to adjust the machine's carburetor and while doing so had indeed dropped a small but vital part, to whit one circlip the size of a five cent piece, which had fallen into the gravel and had since eluded all efforts to locate it. The 4-wheel was useless without it and a replacement was a week away. There was no prospect of anyone talking to me further while the hunt was on, so I joined in.

St. Anthony must have been having an easy morning for as I looked at the gravel there by the toe of my left boot was a small round thing the size of a five cent piece, black with grease and well camouflaged with fine white dust.

I could not believe my luck and hesitated to reveal my find fearing that this was just part of the usual debris that inhabit farm yards, but then held it up, "Is this what you're looking for?" It was, I was surrounded, clapped on the back, shaken by the hand, good luck was called down upon me, my heirs and successors down the ages. I was plied with coffee and scones. The Heysen Trail was granted a right of passage through Mt Falkland Station.

We were happy with our week's work as we drove the long miles home. If only I could solve the Third party liability we would have a major section of trail through the Flinders Ranges.

Apart from persuading the Government to pass a Recreation Trails Act no one could suggest any way of overcoming the problem. There had been a Bill presented to the House of Reps. during the early 1970's but it was largely borrowed from the USA. It was not really appropriate for South Australia and never got a second reading.

It could take years to get an Act through both houses and then there would be no guarantee of success. I had to find another way. What I needed was a simple inexpensive solution that could be put in place quickly, but how?

The whole issue was brought to a head much quicker than any of us expected. The original proposal for the Heysen Trail to continue on past Parachlina Gorge and finally end on the top of Mt Babbage was still the official position at that time and had been since the beginning in 1969. The owners to the north of the Gorge had not taken much notice of the proposal, not really believing it would ever get off the ground. Now quite suddenly the development seemed to be at their front door and they became concerned.

It was the habit of the Department of Agriculture at this time to have a district bureau which met two or three times each year with Departmental officers and other specialists such as scientists and bankers to discuss problems of mutual interest. Such a meeting was called by the Blinman group with only the Heysen Trail on the agenda.

I was invited and it was an invitation I could not refuse, and so I found myself once more headed north to Blinman, much sooner than I had expected.

I had kept in touch with Bill Reschke, a journalist from the Sunday Mail who specialized in reporting on the environment and had a close association with the Trail from the very beginning, and so we arranged to meet in Blinman so that I could show him some of the intended Trail and get some advance publicity. I knew that Bill would report things with an open mind, and that he had already reported on the need for landowners to be protected from claims by walkers. I was also sure that when he saw some of the country we intended the Trail to cross he would argue strongly for more Government action.

I had an answer to all the graziers' concerns with the exception of the most important one. However I did have the embryo of an idea floating around the grey matter.

Sometime before, I had got into a scrap with a landowner over the use of an old unmade road, not on the Heysen Trail but another job I was working on.

There was no doubt that it was a public road with both the fences intact. The owner of the adjoining land claimed to have a lease over the reserve which he claimed extinguished the public's right of passage. A quick check with the District Council produced quite a different story. The landowner had an annual licence over the road for the specific purpose of grazing stock and this did not in any way change the public's right of entry. I went back to the landowner and put the situation to him. He was not happy but accepted defeat. The one thing still bothering him was if that was the case, why did he have to pay the Third party liability insurance premium for the road?

The District Council explained that the holding of a license over the road technically made the licensee the occupier of the land and in law it was the occupier who was responsible for the Third party liability.

This rather convoluted argument was slowly becoming my only hope of salvation. If I could get the State Government to take an annual licence over the Trail then the Government would have the liability. It was with this rather flimsy answer to the problem that I arrived once more in Blinman. I met Bill Reschke who was working on other assignments in the area, and Paul Simpson who held a very senior position in the Department of the Environment on the broad verandah of the pub.

It was still 15 minutes to the appointed time and the landowners were already having a get together inside, no doubt discussing combined tactics. Bill went in to seek them out and get the O.K. for him to attend the meeting in his capacity as a journalist which he soon obtained. Bill spoke to several of the landowners and came back out on to the verandah quite convinced that the Heysen Trail would never become a reality in the Ranges. Such was the opposition from those he had spoken to. I went out of the heat and into the pub, all dark and cool, very quiet with all of the rich malt smells that are the hallmark of pubs just before opening time the world over. The heavy silence was broken only by the distant sound of some far off potman refilling shelves, and the faint silvery tattoo of tables being laid. The meeting was held in the small dining room, dark and still.

The main thrust of the assembly was that they did not want a Heysen Trail on their land, saw no reason for it now or in the future and that it caused them endless problems and expense for absolutely no benefit to them whatsoever. End of story.

Over to me for comment. We got down to the usual details, Fire, gates, litter, camping, lost walkers, my answers reluctantly accepted and then on to, liability - the Achilles heel of all my arguments. We fenced about the subject for a time, then the full focus came on me and I trotted out my half baked scheme. Well perhaps it was the atmosphere of the pub or the pressure or desperation but my annual license scheme sounded a lot better then than it had ever seemed to me before. There were to be many amendments and questions but it was generally believed that this was the answer to the problem. We retired to the now open bar for lunch all jolly good fellows together.

All I had to do now was to sell the scheme to the State Government and make it work.

There were other tasks awaiting me on my return to the office. The initiative on Third party liability was to come from an unexpected source. By some means which I never fully understood. Paul Simpson had brought the plan to Don Hopgood the Minister for the Environment's attention and he had supported it and sent word via my Minister, Jack Slater to me, that he believed the scheme was the answer and would support it if I could get it in to a workable frame work.

Don Hopgood was at this time also Deputy Premier and was proving to be a most effective leader in the field. He was a long time supporter of the Heysen Trail and carried considerable weight in the Cabinet, the body of Government that has to give the final approval to such a radical scheme as this.

With somebody of his eminence offering support there was no time to be lost. I took my case to the Crown Solicitor or at least one of his staff, half expecting to be laughed out of the place. The thing was studied, looked at, passed from hand to hand and various opinions sought. To my great relief they did not clutch their throats, draw the breath in over their teeth while shaking their heads, or invite me to leave.

I was advised to leave the matter with them and they would call me. I had heard plenty of harrowing stories about the long waits while solicitors deliberated, and determined that I was not going to let this happen to me and mentally gave them one week to get back to me. I had no need to worry. Within a few days the solicitor I had seen was on the phone.

I think he must have been a walker, the answer was that it could be made to work and he was putting a proposal in the post which I was to study and then get back to him. Between us we were able to get a submission up to the Cabinet office that worked in this way. Once a land manager had agreed to the Trail being located on his land or over an unmade road that divided a property, the South Australian Government would then take an annual license over the Trail and over a strip of land half a kilometre on ether side of the Trail. The license fee would be one dollar payable on demand. Walkers would not have the right to walk anywhere but on the marked trail and the land managers right to continue to carry on with his normal activities would not be impinged upon.

The only real problem I could find was that a plan showing the Trail and the reserve land had to be produced and if this was to be done by a licensed surveyor the cost would be way out of our range of funding. However our solicitor advised us that providing the plan was acceptable to both parties the standard 1:50,000 Lands Dept. map could be used. The package was now put through the correct channels, first to the senior officers of Recreation, and Sport, then on to the Director, then to our Minister and finally to the Cabinet office, there being questions at each stage. This took time but did ensure that nothing was left to chance if and when it got on to the Cabinet agenda. The next Tuesday, the traditional day that cabinet meets, passed and we did not get up but the following week not only did the Heysen Trail Third party indemnity get on to the agenda but it was approved.

A few weeks later we were on our way back to Blinman with a

Landcruiser and trailer full to the brim with all the necessary signs and posts to mark the Trail from Parachilna Gorge to Wilpena Pound and once again making our base at the Blinman Hotel for the first week. We also had a new crew. Richard Massey had become the victim of his own inventive genius. He had developed the now well known glass terrarium and after a successful sales trip to New Zealand was forced to take up the business full time so as to fulfill the orders which were pressing for delivery. Peter Scapinelli also departed, transferring to the State Transport Authority. Martin took over as supervisor and Bob Bowden and Christine Knight joined the team.

The Blinman Pub had been our home before and once again we settled there. Blinman was a wonderful place at the time of which I write, this being before tourism reached it. The town hardly deserved the description, as the population was only 16, and that if you counted Eric the dog. It was a ramshackle collection of pre 1900 buildings of local stone and timber slowly mouldering into a low hillside at the end of a track leading to Glasses Gorge almost 100km from the Wilpena turnoff.

Blinman's reason for existence had long since ceased, the discovery of a deposit of copper there in the 1860's by a shepherd by the name of Bob Blinman. The story was told to me one night in the pub by a local, I enjoyed it and so have never been motivated to confirm it.

If Robert Blinman was a shepherd then shepherds as a race of people must be remarkably lucky as any sort of mineral find in South Australia always seems to involve some form of animal husbandry. The finder is then always cheated out of his due share by being fobbed off with a five pound note or a bag of magic beans. This was Bob's lot and it was not the only ill fortune to dog our poor Bob.

The fact that he was living in the far north in the 1860's does not say much for his stars. Bob it seems had a wooden leg, at this point the story becomes a little difficult to follow due perhaps to the lateness of the hour. No, he did not collect wooden legs. The one that he owned was to replace the original flesh and bone one that he was first issued with. He was now known as Peg Leg Blinman, shepherd.

He first came to public note when like all good shepherds he was watching his flock by night all seated round the fire, when Bob stretched out his weary limbs and fell asleep, another stroke of bad luck. Bob having stretched out, placed his wooden leg into the flames where it was partially consumed. Whether Bob was able to continue his shepherding career we are not told.

The Pub itself was just as rambling as the village, all stone and wood most of the latter having been painted over many times without going to the nuisance of rubbing down the previous coat. The electrical wiring was a source of great entertainment on dark winter's nights as the inmates bet on the dates of it origin. It always made me feel home-sick as it reminded me of the map of the London underground. The Hotel was built into the hillside so that when you went upstairs to bed you walked out of the back door and you'd be on the ground floor. I suspected that the building had no foundations. My room had a perfectly good solid timber door, a triumph of the joiners art, stout and square but its frame, although stout was anything but rectangular, and would have been more at home in the fun house of lunar park. None of the bedroom doors could ever be shut but it was just one of the building's eccentricities and which we were quite prepared to put up with particularly when Ray and Cheryl were our hosts.

We set out the next morning to begin the marking of the Trail from Parachilna Gorge to Wilpena.

The whole enterprise almost came to an end in the first hour of the first day. We set off along John Henry's mining trail which was in good condition although overgrown by understory. We pushed through, the scrub simply closing behind us seemingly without suffering any harm and we were able to make steady progress for the first hour, then we came to a steep sided gully. This was not a great gorge but simply a creek that had scoured out a course at 90 degrees to the Trail. It was about 20 feet wide at the top and of the same dimension deep, with very steep sides. To the miners, the makers of the Trail this was nothing. They had simply felled the required number of native pine trees and thrown a bridge across the divide. This rude structure had stood the test of time, neither flash flood nor loaded mining carts had weakened it. We went forward on foot to investigate and to check the safety of the structure. We did this using the time honoured method of putting the boot in. No don't scoff this is a sovereign remedy for many an ill. Why I have even known people who when buying a car have spent large sums of money on mechanics, vehicle inspections etc. when the same result could be achieved with a few good kicks at the tyres with a size 10 brogue.

We stepped gingerly out onto the bridge then applied the boot, heel first then the toe. First right foot then the left, and pronounced the structure sound. We returned to the 4-wheeler, each to his appointed place and drove out onto the bridge with quiet confidence. The bridge collapsed in a cloud of rotten wood and dust and fell in a great confusion of bits and pieces to the bottom of the creek, leaving the truck with its front wheels hanging in the air and resting on its belly at a 45 degree angle.

We abandoned the machine with undignified speed through the back doors and retreated down the Trail to review our options. During the previous year John Bannon's Government had begun to take Occupational Health and Safety quite seriously and so Jim Daly and I had been sent off on a series of training courses. At the end of our training we had the strong feeling that John Bannon was going to take the issue seriously and it might not be long before a safety officer was appointed to each department. If this was to happen then the project would be out of the hands of the politicians and handed over to the bureaucrats who would stuff it up.

I therefore decided to appoint Bob Bowden as the outdoor Rec. safety officer to set our house in order so that we would have our procedures in place before we got some public servant who had not been further north than the Gawler Caltex.

Bob was well suited to the position, having worked for 3 years running a drilling rig during the development of the Stuart Highway. This decision was about to pay dividends. We had had the Toyota fitted with a power take off winch and this had worked so well that Bob had persuaded me to find the funding for an electric winch that could be mounted on the rear of the truck as and when required, by a simple device which allowed us to mount the winch on to the tow bar. As for the rest of the time it could be stored out of the way in the back of the wagon.

We considered our options, and over the next hour managed to put the vehicle's handbrake on, start the engine and begin the search for the winch, no mean feat as it had been in the back of the vehicle when we left Blinman that morning and had been bounced about the roads and tracks ever since and was now buried beneath an assortment of way markers, tools and all the other paraphernalia that we carried with us and which by now bore a strong resemblance to the London blitz after a bad night. We got the winch in place and ran out the cable intending to anchor it to a pine.

Native pines grow all over the Flinders hill sides. They grow with the vigour of Soursobs, Paterson's Curse and St. John's Wort; they grow so thickly that they are difficult to walk through and they block the view, and yet there was not one within reach of the end of our cable in any useful direction. Now Bob showed his true worth, producing from some hidden source a coil of sturdy rope, and with this securely fastened to the end of our cable it easily reached a stout pine. The remote control from the winch was now attached and the rewind button pressed and inch by inch this marvelous machine hauled the 37 hundredweight of Landcruiser plus its considerable load up and out of the abyss. We were very relieved. Time and funds were at a premium and if we could not have rescued ourselves the whole exercise might have failed.

As it was we could make no more progress in the 4-wheel and so while I and Martin loaded up our backpacks with waymarkers, tools, radios, food and water, Chris, and Bob set off to drive east and then south and finally west, the 80km to begin marking north towards us.

Our mishap of the first day was the only one of the trip and a combination of early starts and long days saw us marking the Trail into Wilpena on the 11th day. We had all worked very hard and with great dedication, the days had been long but we had been rewarded with perfect weather and one of the most spectacular working environments anywhere.

My satisfaction with our work in the Flinders was short lived however. A week after our return I received a phone call from the Ranger at Wilpena who told me that George Hunt the owner of Wilpena Station was not happy with what I had done. At the time Wilpena Station adjoined the Park on one side immediately to the north of Wilpena Pound. It seemed that Mr Hunt believed I had marked the Trail over part of his lease and was demanding my presence at Wilpena forthwith.

Back on the road; Clare, Wilmington Quorn by night, put up at the Hawker pub and on to meet George Hunt the next morning. George received me with little outward show of his annoyance. From his point of view I was simply a high-handed public servant who had taken the Trail across his leases without even the courtesy of a phone call. George was reasonable about it even suggesting an alternative route; as for the error I still cannot see that it was my fault, George's fences were, as far as I could see, simply in the wrong place and went in the wrong direction. We presented our evidence which was the old game station plan vs. Lands Department map. But I needed George Hunt far more than he needed me and as an alternative was on offer I accepted the blame and apologized, ate the humble and crow pie and donned the sackcloth and ashes. The way was moved with little difficulty staying for longer up on the side of the north wall of the pound, a hard but worthwhile walk full of steep gullies and thick scrub for much of the way.

The whole argument became academic later on when the Wilpena Station lease was bought by the Parks and Wildlife Dept.

Bill Reschke joined us and I conned him into checking the Wilpena to the Wilcola Track section of the Trail with me. The theory was that if Bill could find his way along the path anyone could. There is still an ancient Aboriginal story that the Pound and the surrounding country was made by Arkaroo the great serpent, who after drinking Lake Frome dry made his way down the Flinders, throwing up the Ranges, forming the valleys and then bloated with all the water he had imbibed and exhausted with his labours he coiled up and slept and continues to do so to this day.

His body made the Wilpena Pound and the story goes that he sometimes belches in his sleep, the sound reverberating through the Ranges, As we climbed the rocky ramparts beneath St. Mary's noble

Peak Arkaroo stirred and groaned. Nobody knows what causes the noise, but as Bill said "the vibes were friendly".

On October the 10th 1982 the first Flinders Ranges section of the park opened, this time without fanfare, as our Publicity and Promotions people had decided not to have any more openings until the Trail was completed.

Wonoka to Wilpena

The next obvious section for the Heysen Trail in the Flinders Ranges was to pass though the Pound Gap and cross the inside of the Pound through a series of pine forest, natural clearing and a small thicket of mallee, then easily up the inside of the Pound and on to the Bridle Gap just below Dicks Nob, on the rim of the south wall of the Pound. This easy walk of about 11km is rewarded with some magnificent views. The wall of the Pound drops abruptly away, revealing the Flinders in all its renowned splendour. To the south-east the Chase and Druid Ranges rise and fall in series of reptilian bands wreathed in purple haze. Across the valley 500 feet below lies the Bunbinyunna Range and Black Gap. Across the valley dominating the country is the Elder Range rising buttress upon ochre buttress. I knew this part of the Ranges, having explored much of it whilst working at the old NFC during the 1970's and already knew where the Trail should go.

It had been a vastly different land then; I spent a week on a long rambling back packing trip through this part of the Flinders with an English mate of mine. There must have been a series of good seasons for the land was rich, lush and verdant with even the most minor creeks running with thin strands of crystal water. Now the land was in the grip of a long drought. We climbed down from the Bridle Gap through Blacks Gap and down onto the old travelling stock route now known as the Moralana Drive. The worst of the drought was now apparent, there was not a blade of grass to be seen, the ground was covered in a 2 inch thick blanket of bull dust the consistency of talcum powder. Even the mighty Red Gums in the creeks look stressed. From Blacks Gap to the Hawker road not a living thing was seen, no roos of any kind not a galah or maggie showed itself. I was for once glad to reach the bitumen of the Hawker Road and turn south for home.

From the edge of the Pound, the country for almost 40km south to Mayo Gorge is on a perpetual Lease, which gives its lease holder almost all of the rights of a freehold landowner. Arkaba is one of the old historic pastoral runs and takes its name from the Aboriginal people of the district. It was still early as we made our way towards Hawker and on a whim I asked Andrew to stop at Arkaba's gate, and then to take us 2km to the station. Something was wrong. No bevy of dogs came out to meet us, the old stone sheds, usually the centre of

An old miner's hut near Blinman

activity on most properties were darkly silent, no-aged utes, 4-wheel drives or ag-bikes dotted the scene. I left the other two in the truck and started off to the homestead, fought the usual battle with the gate and its patented easy opening, self closing latch that had not worked in living memory and had been reinforced with liberal quantities of black bailing twine. I walked hesitatingly up the garden path where a few rank Geraniums struggled valiantly to put on a show. I reached the front door and found it wide open. Only the fly screen barred the way. The passage was too dark for my eyes to penetrate; I was rapidly changing my mind, this piece of impetuousness no longer seemed like such a good idea. I decided to do the honorable thing and flee, but before I could turn there came from deep within the sound of stirring then a bold "hello" and I was face to face with Mr Bartholomews the owner of the lease. Batholomews was a large shambling man of ample girth clad in a brown rather snug fitting boiler suit. He greeted me in a friendly way and invited me in leading the way down the nocturnal passage and into a well lit spacious lounge. I was offered coffee and accepted. Mr Bartholomews departed to another part of the house leaving me to assess my surroundings which were strange indeed. The first thing to take my eye was that the well carpeted floor was strewn with portions of plumbing, including a partly dissassembled toilet system, its attendant parts and the necessary tools of the plumber's art. Then there were spread about the room on various tables, a series of obviously expensive books. All open and face up with glossy full plate color prints of some far off sunny clime possibly the Mediterranean or the Aegean sea. Mr Bartholomews returned with coffee before I could investigate further. We made our mutual introductions and my host explained the property was so badly drought stricken that all the stock had been sold off and the staff sent to Adelaide. The poor chap had been living on the place alone and to pass the time he had been maintaining the plumbing and studying Greek culture. I explained my mission and it was received very favourably. The route I described on the map was quickly accepted with the proviso that Batholomews be allowed to ride his trail bike along the Trail. So the deal was done, in less that an hour we had added over 40km to the Trail. A distance that in other circumstances would take months. I wished Mr Bartholomews all the best for the future. I felt rather sorry for the bloke as the future was obviously not a good prospect for him. During the next few weeks we had a good look at the country from Mayo Gorge down to Wonoka Creek on the Hawker to Copley road and found another travelling stock route that would make the connection. We met Tony McGuinness who owned the Wonoka station, the adjoining property, who happily gave us his support, and within a few weeks we were back marking the Trail from Wilpena across the Pound through Bridle Gap across the Morlana Drive and got as far as the remains of Umberutna, which took 3 of us 5 days. We also taped the way between the Red Range up Beatrice Creek to the water shed then down to Mayo Gorge following Slaty and then Mernmerna Creeks. We met the Adelaide Bush Walkers on the Saturday morning at the Hawker road crossing. ABW had volunteered to do the marking and mapping from there to the Moralana Drive.

The Heysen Trail was now 600km long, 200km through the Flinders Ranges. A few months later Arkaba was put up for sale.

Quorn to Wonoka

Despite the difficulty with the reserve over Mt Brown and the problem of finding $35,000 to survey the route we would not give up the proposed up-route, it was just too good and the alternative was a walk along a little used back road. So we decided to continue the development of the Trail from the summit of Mt Brown north towards Quorn and trust to our luck that something would turn up. The Heysen Trail had always been lucky, it had become a joke amongst the staff. The patron saint of walkers who ever that might be, did not let us down. Relief was close at hand and that hand belonged to John Porter, President of the Institute of Surveyors, who upon hearing of our plight once again came to the rescue with an offer for his members to undertake the work if the Dept. paid their expenses. The offer was accepted without hesitation. We were soon able to mark the route up to the summit of Mt Brown. Much of this work was done by Andrew and Martin and once more they ran into a patch of rare bad weather carrying the job through in torrential rain and freezing conditions.

There was still opposition from some landowners. This came soon enough in a very physical form, within weeks of the marking being complete the way markers were pulled out and carried away. However we quickly did the marking again and this time it stayed, this was largely due to the outrage that the greater part of the community expressed at the vandalism.

We were now looking at the final long stretch of the Trail from Woolshed Flat to the Hawker Road just south of Wonoka Station.

This would mean crossing several of the old historic grazing runs, the Pichi Richi Railway and the Dutchman's Stern Conservation Park. This would take us into contact with some of the most interesting characters we had yet met. I was awarded a Churchill Fellowship at this time and was absent overseas for four months, leaving at first Martin Foster and then Andrew Moylan in charge of the project. Andrew worked prodigiously while I was away and must have spent most of the two months that he was in charge in the Quorn district. The result of this was that there was no let up in the progress being made and things were well advanced by the time I returned in the October of 1991. The Trail descends the northern ridge of Mt Brown where it finds its way into the valley of Wucary Creek which runs west to cross the Stirling North to Quorn road. The way then turns once again north climbing very steeply up to the summit of a ridge. This property was owned by Robert Miller and Eleanor Spice. Eleanor was from a family with a long history of grazing in this far flung reach of the State. She was one of the most enthusiastic landowners I had ever met. We always got a warm welcome from Eleanor, usually with tea and scones at which Eleanor presided, always the perfect host and always elegantly and appropriately dressed for the occasion. Eleanor gave us not only help but urged us on to finish the Trail. When the Trail was finally finished in 1993 Ms Spice had no hesitation in accepting the invitation to attend the opening ceremony, driving 300km to do so.

We received great help on this piece of Trail but even so It turned out to be one of the hardest sections to mark. The ranges here are precipitous and the way markers, tools, food and water had to be backpacked up and over one of these steep scrub covered ridges of unstable shale. Ms Spice allowed us to take our 4-wheeled drives as close as we could get but even so it was a long and back breaking job and the volunteers did well to see it through. We had some very strong supporters in the Quorn district, I was happy to find Bob West an old mate from the Clayton Outward Bound School days running the outdoor school in the town. Bob was also the captain of the State

Emergency Service, and so knew the country well and also many of the landowners, and so was able to save us a huge amount of time. The Quorn School too was eager to help and the senior master Mr Camel, with the blessing of parents, organized the students into a work force. One farming Dad even had a set of old pack saddles and several work horses were produced from around the District and they did a lot of the carrying of markers up the north side of Mt Brown

The property to the north of the Spice place was run by a chap called Doug Kite and I got a less favourable response from him at first but persisted. After pointing out that there was a public road crossing his land connecting it with the Pichi Richi Railway reserve, Doug agreed to meet me on the property so that I could show him exactly where we wanted to locate the Trail. Doug insisted that I ride with him in his 4-WD ute and we were soon chatting away like old mates. "I heard you on the wireless last week Terry, you been to China?" I confirmed that I had. "What's the beer like over there" asked Doug. "Its a good drop" I answered. We got on fairly well after that and the route was agreed although there was no great joy expressed by Mr Kite and I knew that we would have to play the game with great care if we were going to keep the way open. Doug went about his business and I rejoined my mates and we got ourselves organized to get the marking underway. This was in contrast with the previous section, and we made good progress through some classic Flinders creeks and about 3:30 in the afternoon joined a 4-WD track that was the main connecting track between the Kite homestead and the road to Quorn. This way would take the Trail east to join with the railway reserve. It had been an exceptionally wet winter in the Ranges and the ground if not yet boggy would soon become impassable following heavy rains, and Doug had already warned us about the delicate state of his tracks. The weather was not looking good, the sun had gone and with it the small warmth of the day. The sky had become leaden and an early night seemed promised. We hurried on hoping to get the thing over and back to the comfort of the pub. The only difficulty we might have was a long steep section of bench out track which ran uphill for about 1.2km.

We marked the Trail on the southern side of the track and were soon at the top where we met Doug Kite heading home with his tray top full of ewes. He asked me how the marking was going and I foolishly invited him to inspect our handy work. This he did, and after a short perusal proclaimed it to be unsatisfactory; 'it should' said our benefactor 'be marked on both sides of the track'. We turned the Landcruiser and went back to the bottom of the hill leaving men and markers at strategic points along the way, and started once more up from the bottom of the incline marking as we went. But by this time the rain was beginning to sluice down. We managed to get about two thirds up the slope, we were almost home but when we attempted to start up the final section of the hillside the vehicle refused to move, unable to get a grip on the saturated ground. We decided to unhitch the trailer in the belief that it was the trailer's weight that was stopping our uphill progress. The trailer's wheels were carefully blocked up with wedge shaped rocks and having done this we unhitched it. The trailer did not hesitate, it rode up and over the rocks and set off down the track enjoying its first taste of freedom. At first the trailer took a fairly straight course down the hillside but soon after it turned diagonally across the track, then reaching its maximum speed, it launched itself off the track and into mid air above the adjoining creek where it made a perfect landing some 50 metres below. It was now almost dark and raining heavily. We climbed back on board the Landcruiser which relieved of the burden of the trailer, took us easily up the hill and to the pub. By 10pm the rain had stopped and the sky was clear. The next morning the sun was shining down and there was no sign of the downpour of the night before. We drove back to salvage the wreck of the trailer, but after we had winched it out of the creek bed and back on to the track we found it undamaged, hitched it up to the 4-WD, finished the job on Doug Kite's place and went on to the next task. During all this time in the Quorn area we made our Headquarters at the Criterion Hotel run by Mal and Jan who always treated us very well. Mal with rough good humor was the spitting image of Sergeant Cryer straight out of the British police show 'The Bill'. and Jan always concerned with our comfort, often asking us for suggestions for the Pub menu.

On one notable occasion we had a large group of about 15 volunteers, working in a series of creeks to the south of Mt Arden and finishing in Depot Creek. Three weeks before I had investigated the route from the south, walking north from Dutchmans Stern CP through some very steep and tortuous country and had got to Depot Flat about an hour before dark just in time to be picked up by 4-WD and taken home. This left a few kilometres of the proposed Trail unexplored. I decided that we would go ahead with the marking even though I had not investigated it beforehand. I did take the precaution however, of discussing the route with landowner Kevin Fitzgerald the night before and he advised me go easy as there were three waterfalls on the lower part of the creek. We transported the party onto the lower slopes of Mt Arden then split up into groups, me with one group going in front taping the route that I wanted marked, a second party putting way markers in place, another group back packing in way markers from our depot at the beginning of the creek; while a third small group glued the logos and directional markers onto the waymarkers. It was in this fashion that I intended to complete the marking of Mt Arden Creek, but of course things did not go the way I had planned. The creek shown on the map was not the one that was on the ground; somehow the map makers had got it in a muddle and put the wrong one on the map Just how they can do this with all their expensive equipment, I failed to comprehend, not that I minded for myself you understand, I am used to it. I am experienced in such things, but what about the poor fellow who has got my creek. How is he going to get on? Then the compass started playing up, it was one of those foreign imports which I suppose is alright for the northern hemisphere where there are sign posts every few yards and milestones scattered all over the place, and there are always policemen standing about just longing to be asked for directions or the time and waiting to be told how wonderful they are.

Spring Creek in flood

In South Australia we needed something more substantial, more reliable, something more in keeping with our rugged wide brown land. Now this imported thing would not point where I wanted it to point, and have you noticed that in this situation every one within miles suddenly becomes the world's greatest navigator and begins plying you with worthless advice? It is the same when your car breaks down, lift the hood of the car and suddenly everyone becomes a motor mechanic. I put the compass in my pocket cursing the English sister-in-law who sent it to me. It had been my intention not to stay in the bed of the creek as it followed a rather serpentine course, almost at times doubling back on itself, and so to progress 5kms in a straight line the Trail would have had to cover twice that distance. My intention was to cut the corners and bends, thereby saving considerable distance with the added advantage that the Trail would not take the walker over a difficult boulder strewn creek bed for the whole journey. At first this ploy worked well enough. However we soon found ourselves getting into more of a gorge rather than just a creek bed, not that the sides towered above us , not at first anyway, but just high and steep enough to make climbing out of the creek difficult, time consuming and just a bit hazardous. So we were forced to walk the whole winding way, with the sides of the creek getting higher and higher until they finally became a true gorge. Well at least we would not run out of markers and have to return to the job the next day. This was, of course due to the fact that there was no way to leave the creek and walkers would be forced to follow it regardless of way markers. It was late in the afternoon when we came across the first of Mr Fitzgerald's waterfalls, of which I had by this time forgotten. The fall was not much more than a flight of steep steps easily negotiated by the party, and we went on in good spirits and with high expectations of an early finish after all. Now the second fall presented itself, 30ft deep worn smooth and almost sheer, we got down it without difficulty but it took time and when we were all assembled at the bottom the light was almost gone. However we had only a short distance to go to reach our vehicles. After dropping us off at Mt Arden Creek the drivers had been told to meet us at Depot Flat in the afternoon and it was not long before we met them coming up the creek to meet us. This was not however to be a joyous reunion for they had inspected the third waterfall and in the failing light had found it to be impossibly high, steep and overhanging. They had found a safer way around, this by climbing out of the gorge and then high over the ridge to the east of the waterfall.

This was done but mostly in the dark and it took almost two hours to get us all safely down to the 4-WDs. One more problem faced us, the track that the vehicles had come by was no longer in use, being very difficult, steep winding and in bad repair. I had travelled it in daylight only the month before and was not prepared to use it now by night.

The only alternative was to go west out on to the plains and on a drive that took us almost into the back streets of Port Augusta. I led a very tired and shame-faced group of walkers into the bar that night, it was 10pm, just four hours late for our dinner. We stood and waited for the well deserved retribution, but we were only met with concerns for our well being and safety. Then we were hustled off to wash our hands while our 3 course dinner was served. The three months that we took to develop the Trail between Dutchmans Stern and the Hawker Road were certainly the most intensive of any we had throughout the development of the Heysen Trail. There were many reasons for this. We had been on the project for over 14 years and at last could see an end to it. The Friends of the Heysen Trail were operating with their largest membership, enthusiasm had never been higher, the volunteers were well trained.

Heysen Trail

Mrs HUTCHINSON (Sturt): Will the Minister of Recreation and Sport give the House an update on the development of the Heysen Trail? Will the Minister also inform the House what is the proposed time table for its completion?

The Hon. M.K.MAYES: I thank the Honourable member for Stuart for her question, because that this issue is very dear to her. Certainly, as member of that district, I am sure that she will be delighted to be a participant in the opening of the Trail — which, I hope, is not too far away.

I am pleased to inform the House that the final section of the Heysen Trail between Woolshed Flat — which I am sure is well known to the honourable member and which is near Quorn --- and Hawker is currently under construction. In the past few months, our team in the section of the department, plus many people from the Friends of the Heysen Trail, have been working together to complete the section of over 130km. I have been provided with information about markers, warning and information signs, buildings, bridges, stiles, fences, and all the erosion barriers, which are very important in all those areas because of the need to ensure that farmers land is protected. In particular, we must ensure that stock are not injured or damaged in any way by the activity, especially later when walkers have access.

There has been cooperation between the Department landowners and district councils. I want to thank the district councils because without their cooperation and support, we would not have achieved the end result. I hope that a formal opening will take place in October this year.

The time table is set for October when we will be able to open the whole of the Heysen Trail. I think that it will be unique, because I am sure it will attract not only many South Australians but also many overseas visitors. It will also bring in many interstate visitors. It is becoming one of the major outdoor assets of this State and nationally it is recognised for what it will provide in terms not only of recreation but of opportunities for people to see South Australia from another aspect. I thank the honourable member for her question and look forward to the opening in October.

This part of the Trail was some distance from Adelaide and so I had to budget for overnight expenses for both the full time workers and volunteers. I had also to hire additional 4-WDs and it was imperative that we get the most out of the resources we had while we had them. We often had 20 volunteers based at Quorn working in 5 day shifts, often these were broken into three work parties and moving them from work site to work site took some juggling, plus it left no vehicle spare during the day for visits to landowners to sort out last minute problems and these had to be done at night, which put great strain on some of the staff.

The volunteers also put up with many difficulties without complaint. On only one occasion did we have more groups than usual, but were restricted to just three 4-WDs. At the end of one long hard shift we found that somehow we had contrived to leave one of our groups sitting on a ridge top for 3 hours, not on a typical Flinders sunny afternoon but on one of the wettest and coldest in living memory. It never happened again. Andrew Moylan probably got the worst deal out of it, having acted in my place for 2 months he had spent a lot of time with the landowners and got to know them, and while I was absent and Andrew acted in my position he drew my pay which was fair enough, the problem was when I came back he immediately reverted to his substantive position and it was not simply a matter of him stopping the negotiations , landowners do not like their contacts changing half way though the process.

The way from Doug Kites' was certainly spectacular. We had to get the path through the ranges and down into Depot Flat and this we did by enlisting the help of the Ranger in charge of the district, Shirley Myers. I had met Shirley many years before when she was an office assistant in the Port Lincoln office of the Parks and Wildlife Service and she had battled her way up the ranks which was no mean feat. We sought Shirley's help to take the path through the Dutchmans Stern Conservation Park which was under her control. This was done after negotiations with Shirley in her forthright and robust way. The Trail passed over the summit of Mt Arden, there are views in every direction which cannot be bettered anywhere that I have ever walked or climbed. From Mt Arden the way swings across wide valleys and over ridges of fractured stone past stations with strange sounding names like Buckaringa, Partacoona, The Oaks and many others owned or managed by the likes of Ian Smart, Len Dear, John Rowe, Graham Stokes and John Walmsley. Finally over the red stone ribs of Jarvis Hill with more spectacular panoramas sweeping north to the Wilpena Pound and down to the Hawker Road past Yappala there to join with the already completed parts of the Heysen Trail.

The Last Post

And so the last post was put into place.

The Heysen Trail was complete, a continuous footpath from Cape Jervis to Parachilna Gorge a distance of 1,500km, the equivalent of walking from London to Madrid or Chicago to New Orleans. Completed under budget and four years ahead of time. The longest footpath in the world. For 15 years the development had gone on, for most of that time with just one public servant, never more than three permanent staff and a host of volunteers. Between us we had made, carted and erected more than 12,000 waymarkers, manufactured and installed over 4,500 stiles, routed and painted 8000 warning and information signs, built bridges, sand ladders, board walks, designed and authored 15 maps, 2 books and a mass of information and advisory pamphlets, coordinated the efforts of 18 Government departments and offices and obtained the goodwill of hundreds of rural landowners and district councils.

We had, without so called professional help, put South Australia on the international walking map and in airline inflight magazines, newspapers and trade journals.

The Heysen Trail and its makers received two major tourism awards and became recognized in this country and overseas as the leaders in the development of outdoor recreation facilities. For 20 years the Heysen Trail had the support of Governments from all sides of the political spectrum. As one newspaper put it, we had created the jewel in South Australia's tourism crown. It is barely 6 years since The Premier, Lynn Arnold declared the entire Heysen Trail open, yet in that brief time the Trail has gone from the newspapers; its existence under threat, the volunteers are disillusioned, the experienced staff have been dispersed. However I do not despair of the Trail's future; there is still a fierce love of bushwalking and of the Heysen Trail concept. There remains a hardcore group of supporters who will rise once again to the challenge to rebuild the Trail when the Authorities wake up to themselves as soon they surely must.

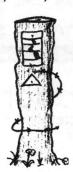

Terry Lavender AO

Our boots are made for walking

And that's just what they do

On the Heysen, the Larapinta or the
Appalachian Trail

Mount Lofty, Mount Kosciusko,
or Mount Everest

In Rundle Street, Old Kent Road or Fifth Avenue

The Snowgum Outdoor Centre has footwear for
all Outdoor pursuits.

They are fitted by Outdoor people who won't
let you go out of the store with ill fitting boots.

That's our money back guarantee.

Snowgum Outdoor Centre
192 Rundle Street Adelaide SA 5000

The Walking Federation of South Australia Inc.

The Walking Federation of SA, known as Walking SA, is the peak body for recreational walking in South Australia. With the support of affiliated bushwalking clubs, and individual members, the Federation works in the following ways to enhance walking opportunities in South Australia.

- *Ensures that access to walking areas remain open.*
- *Provides information on walking opportunities to members and the general public.*
- *Maintains a resource centre with useful information to walkers.*
- *Negotiates with relevant government agencies on walking related issues.*
- *Assists with insurance for clubs.*
- *Publishes a quarterly newsletter detailing items of interest to walkers in SA.*

By joining the Federation you can add strength to our efforts.

- Club Membership is $40.00 per year
- Individual Membership is $18.00 per year
  (which includes a quarterly Newsletter)

for more details telephone our office or visit our website

Walking SA Office

2 Union Street, Stepney, **Telephone** 8363 6955
(Office open Monday & Thursday)

Postal address PO Box 509, Stepney, SA 5069
email office@walkingsa.org.au
website www.walkingsa.org.au

South Australian Recreation Trails Inc.

This is a community initiative comprising several local government authorities, the Scout Association, Walking Federation of SA, and a number of other community based Organisations.

Up to date, all walking trails have been supported by the Government, but now, the walking community and the general populace should be prepared to continue with the development of these trails, which are a great asset to South Australia.

THE FEDERATION TRAIL, when completed, will run from Murray Bridge to Clare, and will be the first long distance countryside walking trail implemented by the community.

People interested in this South Australian venture are encouraged to register their support.

For more information:
contact Bob Schroder of SARTI on (08)8532 1288
or mobile: 0412 816 441

On your Way to the Last Post
Make your First Footprints with Pathfinders

First Footprints is the entry level bushwalking group in the Pathfinder Adventure Program. There are *Pathfinder* walks for general level bush walkers and *Trekkers* for those looking for a bigger challenge.

Groups are limited to 15 people. The professional leaders are chosen for their outdoor skills and ability to make walking a pleasure for the group.

Contact Snowgum for a program.
Address: 192 Rundle Street, Adelaide, 5000
Ph: 8223 5544
Email: soc@scoutnet.net.au